# Oh My Mother!

# Oh My Mother!

### A MEMOIR IN NINE ADVENTURES

## Connie Wang

VIKING

VIKING
An imprint of Penguin Random House LLC
penguinrandomhouse.com

Photos on pages 214 and 215 from the collection of Qing Li and Dexin Wang.

LIBRARY OF CONGRESS CATALOGING-IN-PUBLICATION DATA
Names: Wang, Connie, author.
Title: Oh my mother! : a memoir in nine adventures / Connie Wang.
Description: New York : Viking, [2023]
Identifiers: LCCN 2022057609 (print) | LCCN 2022057610 (ebook) |
    ISBN 9780593490921 (hardcover) | ISBN 9780593490938 (ebook)
Subjects: LCSH: Wang, Connie. | Authors—Biography. |
    Asian American women authors—Biography. |
    Wang, Connie—Family. | Mothers and daughters.
Classification: LCC HQ755.85 .W36 2023 (print) |
    LCC HQ755.85 (ebook) | DDC 306.874/3—dc23/eng/20221206
LC record available at https://lccn.loc.gov/2022057609
LC ebook record available at https://lccn.loc.gov/2022057610

Printed in the United States of America
1st Printing

*Designed by Amanda Dewey*

献给姥爷

# Contents

# INTRODUCTION

In Chinese, the closest expression to *oh my god* is *wǒde mā ya*. It's an interjection. A polite expletive. Something to say when you're out of words. But there's no god present in the phrase, and I like the Chinese version better, because it feels more like the truth. Translated literally, it means *oh my mother*—the first person I think of when I'm on the cusp of losing it, or putting it all together.

I think about my own mother, Qing Li, so often that I feel it must be unhealthy. I think about her reflexively (*I wish she were here right now* / *I wonder what she's doing* / *I should call her*) but also deliberately and resolutely, imagining all five foot two of her standing in front of me, scrutinizing what I'm doing. I find myself thinking about Qing when I do anything new, when I do anything I realize has become routine. I think about her when I encounter exotic ideas, exciting situations, and unbearable emotions. Periodically, despite my best efforts, I write down these thoughts for others to read. I say *despite* because she is not someone I ever wanted to write about, because to write about your mom, especially if it's your job to write, is to reveal that you have nothing much to write about in the first place. After all, in the vastness and pastness of human history, one of the few universal truths is that everyone has a mom, and everyone feels some sort of way about her. On a more specific front, it's entirely too obvious for a first-generation East Asian immigrant to have a filial piety complex, to loiter in a mother-shaped shadow. And yet I have continued to put my thoughts about Qing on paper, over and over, in published essays and Instagram captions; in texts with friends who are forever inquiring after her; in reported pieces I wrote as a journalist, in which quoting your own mother is usually about as constructive (or impressive) as bringing a teddy bear to battle.

By force of personality, influence, and blood, my mother has been the angel and the devil on my shoulders, the little voice in my head, and the creative muse that I have pushed against and climbed upon.

This book is an attempt to explain my fascination with my mother, who is by many measures a very ordinary woman. She still lives in the same suburban home my sister and I grew up in, and has held a position as an accountant at the same company that's employed her for more than twenty-five years. She has been married to my father for thirty-five years, and had two kids who grew up to be, by most standards, perfectly fine. This vision of her, and of the four of us, is what used to dominate my understanding of myself as the product of a pattern: as a member of a lonely Chinese family inside a two-story build-a-home, each of us playing our roles exactly as written—the engineer father perpetually beleaguered at work, the tiger mom with a temper, the prickly elder daughter, and the rebellious baby sister. There was a glossy black piano in the living room and plastic wrap on the remote control, and bills were opened the day they arrived in the mail.

The normalcy of this side of Qing sits in contrast to her diverse eccentricities, character quirks I long assumed were formed out of an internal need to be seen as one of a kind. (A recurring theme of this book, if you'll allow me a bit of a spoiler, is that I am wrong about a lot, especially when it comes to her.) Qing has always insisted that she was uncategorizable by either personality tests or astrological designation—that she had more in common with the celebrities of the world than with the other moms who dropped off their kids for Chinese school on Saturdays. Her body naturally fits into runway fashion samples. Her favorite meal is two crème brûlées. Even when she was a child, born the youngest and frailest of her family during the last year of

China's Great Leap Forward, her refined tastes meant that all the rationed white sugar, sesame paste, and eggs went to fancy, feeble, fussy Qing Li. Her peculiar philosophies—why townhouses are bad investments (snakes in the walls); why Scandinavians are the noblest of white people (universal healthcare); why Drumstick ice cream cones are a healthy breakfast option (there are nuts—more on all of that later)—burrow into the brains of any who hear them, little disruptive prods against logic, sense, and fact.

I first started writing about Qing during a period in the 2010s when the personal essay had become pervasive. Those days, it seemed like every story was in some way a story about identity—the search for it, the lack of it, the compulsion over projecting it, presenting it, and having it be reflected back by others, magazine covers, and television shows. Especially in my line of work, first as a fashion editor and then as a writer at an online publication geared toward women on the fringes, everyone was obsessed with finding themselves and for others to see and hear and affirm the selves they found. I was familiar with the search; I had been looking my entire life. There was a place, I imagined, where my tastes, my ambitions, my struggles, and my values were everyone else's, too. I read voraciously, hoping to find the treasure map in text, and I watched TV looking for myself, for a clue about someplace I could go where life could be more than eating, sleeping, and studying—more than just performing the mechanics of living. That era of my life could be described as a professionally sanctioned, personally motivated search for belonging, and it took me to the farthest coasts I could manage, in dizzying circles around the globe, to dinner tables and neighborhoods and closed rooms and wide-open spaces whose only common denominator was its foreignness to me. But the cumulation of these trips I've taken, with Qing either next to me in the passenger seat or just on my mind, have shown me that my search was doomed, at least in the approach I initially took. I'm excited to tell you why.

During those years, I wrote about Qing in what I now see as a dishonest way. The facts were true, but the motivations were mine. How I portrayed her, as wise and resilient, a victim and a curiosity, was how I genuinely understood her—as a projection of myself. The truth is that I did not understand her then, as I was preoccupied with understanding myself. And after writing a book about her, I know with some certainty that I do not understand her now.

But there is a difference between then and now, I swear. This book is about the difference.

Before I first presented Qing with the idea of this book, I was unsure of how she would react. Would she be flattered? Upset? Her response surprised me: "People want to hear about immigrants' suffer," she said, her brows sinking into deep rivulets. "You know, Mama is boring. No bad things happen. Just weird . . . ideas."

Since then, I have had a thousand conversations about those weird ideas, and the circumstances through which they were formed. I have gotten to know that *no bad things* was a rose-colored statement, and have come to see why Qing chooses to approach her life this way. This is our memoir—a long personal essay, if you will—and it was forged through shared fact-checking: Qing was the first person to read each chapter as it was written, and she is this book's first editor. Every word you read here has first passed under her red pen.

In witnessing Qing's involvement in telling her own story, of the sections where she challenged my recollections and the places where she gave me elbow room to paint the picture on my own, I am convinced that her story is the best response to her own pessimistic assumption that all folks want from immigrants are tragic tales of trauma—or happy assurances that everything is fine, that the American Dream is still on offer. Her story is captivating not because of the hijinks or catastrophes, of which there are many, or in the happily ever afters, of which there are also many, but rather because of her capacity to forever change, evolve, and surprise.

Put simply, this is a book about the noteworthy places we've visited—both physical and otherwise—and what we've gotten out of them, the intangible souvenirs of our sated curiosities: the opportunities to shuck lies from their shells, to glimpse futures that could (or could never) have been ours, to give us a real reason to be angry with each other in order for us to share why we had been angry with ourselves. Trip by trip, I came to understand that my mother was indeed one of a kind, just like she's always insisted. And she, with some tens of thousands of miles behind her, came to see that the humble life she had found herself living has been nothing short of a triumph.

Oh My Mother!

# Prologue

*I*'m supposed to be meeting my mom in America," I told her in Mandarin at the airport. I was two, old enough to talk but too young to remember who she was, despite the fact that just six months prior, I had spent every day of my life with her. "*Is my mom you?*"

"*That's me,*" Qing responded, asking if it was all right if she held me. In her arms, I was much heavier than she expected. But then again, everything in America had been heavier, harder, and dirtier than how she remembered things in China. Back in Jinan, Qing had been a college-educated book editor at a prestigious publishing house, with an influential family, close friends, and an apartment filled with pretty things she bought with her own money. Her new husband had promised her that America was going to be even better. But here in Nebraska, she had no job—she picked up odd shifts at a Chinese restaurant that served disgusting food, busing instead of waitressing, because to waitress, she would need a better command of English. And now her daughter was here, too, to join her on this never-ending vacation from hell.

IT WAS a miracle that my father made it to the United States at all. Dexin had come to attend graduate school, a still-new concept for my parents' generation, who were born during China's violent Great Leap Forward and subsequent Cultural Revolution, which took place from the 1950s through the 1970s, when many intellectuals, my grandparents among them, were sent to labor camps, universities and institutions were shut down, and higher education was denounced as a dangerous distraction.

After Mao's death, post-secondary schools in China reopened all at once. Both Dexin and Qing were among this pioneer class of students, though they didn't meet until after they had both graduated. Qing was working as a junior editor of nonfiction at a well-respected publishing firm when a friend of hers introduced her to Dexin, a stoic and awkward man with hooded eyes and tan arms that were thin and muscled, like stalks of beef jerky. Their relationship was romantic, and they complemented each other; she was fearless and straightforward, unafraid to say exactly what was on her mind, and he was careful and shy (in the beginning of their courtship, Dexin didn't make eye contact with Qing until she threatened to break up with him). They eloped, as was the trend among tradition-averse young people at the time, based on a mutual commitment that he would ensure their survival and she would ensure they'd enjoy their life together.

Children, in Qing's eyes, did not fit into the calculus of a life spent thriving, but when she became pregnant despite the birth control pills she was on, my grandmother convinced her to forgo an abortion. *I think a child would be good for you*, Qing was told, not receiving any further explanation.

Months later, I was born. I was neither big nor small, neither a terrible burden nor a hard-won blessing. A modestly sized slice of plenty. My name, Xiaokang (小康), given to me by my grandfather, referred to the Communist Party commitment to achieving "a moderately prosperous society": 小康社会. The Chinese Dream of modest, basic comforts for all. A dream that, by the same token, rejects luxurious extravagances for the few.

IT MIGHT SEEM PHONY to describe Qing's childhood as luxurious, but it was for her. She was born during the end of a three-year streak of natural and planned disasters, a time when millions of people resorted to eating their own belts and boiling tree bark before starving to death. Sickly and so small, Qing was fed the fattiest cuts of life: all of the family's allotment of rationed peanuts and tart disks of hawthorn candy, tender attention from her elders and neighbors, and freedom from having ever to do chores. When she was three, Qing's parents, who both worked full-time at a state-owned book publishing company, managed to enroll her in an expensive daycare program, but she was expelled after a week. The caregivers explained that she took so long to eat her lunch that it was disruptive to the other children, who agreeably and easily fell into the strict schedule. "*She's not special*," the daycare owner explained to Qing's parents, which was the end of the discussion, and so they were forced to ask a distant aunt to move in with them to help. This aunt, an iconoclast with infinite patience and no temper to speak of, let Qing make her own decisions and do things at her own pace.

Qing has since proclaimed that she never recovered from this initial spoiling, carrying her self-centeredness and her penchant for treats into her adulthood. After graduating and getting her job at the publishing house, she and her best friend, Li Yu, would blow their entire monthly paychecks all in one weekend, on restaurants and asymmetrical haircuts, on fashion magazines, lipsticks, and clothes her father forbade her to wear around him, like tight jeans and billow-ing striped shirts and bug-eyed sunglasses that made her look like the future. A part of her felt guilty, but people ex-pected this kind of coddled foolishness from her, including her new husband.

So when a new door opened to Dexin—a chance to get a doctorate degree abroad—Qing said yes even though she doubted out loud that it was anything but a brief diversion. The Chinese government had recently allowed a small frac-tion of its new student class to apply to schools abroad in fields in which its young citizens could be reliably competi-tive and subsequently useful to the state. Dexin chose an applied physics program to study a deliciously new tech-nology, nanomagnetics, at the University of Nebraska in Lincoln—a town that had enjoyed some notoriety in China because the school's president was a good friend of the senior George Bush, and made it a point to foster warm relations with the country because he was gunning for a diplomat position. Dexin even liked how the name of the university sounded: presidential, American.

The plan was that Dexin would first go by himself. He would complete his PhD degree in four years (he had heard of people doing it in as few as three, if they focused), and then wash his hands of America. If all went well, Qing would join him for part of the time he was there, but she was in no rush. She had better things to do at home, including a job that suited her professional skills and her proclivities. At this point she had been promoted to associate editor; she went on business trips to attend conventions and meet with famous writers, and after the business of the day, she would eat ice cream bars by herself in hotel rooms, and felt very fancy and satisfied. She didn't know anyone as young as she was who took trips like these. It was all very modern. And it was happening all at once—a real career, a child, a husband with promise—and what a good stroke of luck it was that each new step allowed her to preserve her own independence, her shopaholism, her right to have her whims and follow them wherever.

Dexin left in January 1988 with a borrowed fifty dollars (he spent one dollar on a ninety-seven-cent Coke at the airport during a layover in San Francisco—he had told the cashier, with misguided pride, "Three cents is your tip."). A university professor introduced him to a white family in a quiet, historic part of Lincoln to help him acclimate; Jon and Doris were a charitable couple who mentored a rotating crew of Chinese students like my dad on where to go to buy groceries, how to celebrate the Fourth of July, and why there was no shame in accepting money for odd jobs. Rent in America was obscene—hundreds of American dollars a month when his work-subsidized apartment in China was just one yuan, the equivalent of thirty cents—and so he found boarding at the Little White House, which is what the Chinese students who lived in the student cooperative called it, and paid sixty-five dollars a month to sleep in the living room of a unit with an older student who took the only bedroom, and who made long-distance phone calls throughout the night and ate asparagus fried in the same unwashed pan every day.

The next year, in March, my father bought a one-way plane ticket for $1,400 and mailed it to my mother, but the envelope ended up stuck in Beijing because no one at the post office knew what to make of the English letters on the front. Qing's older sister, Li Bai, came with her to Beijing with a quick-tongued boss in tow in case some official needed to be convinced that it was all right to allow Qing to fly to America.

Neither Qing nor Dexin knew how long her visit to America would last. It was all very confusing as they figured out their future together. But Qing knew this much for sure: If Dexin's degree would take four years to get, then she'd take a four-year vacation in America, but that was it. They'd be back. After she retrieved the ticket, Qing made arrangements with her parents so that they could watch me while she was away, and then she met with her editor in chief to quit. The editor in chief told Qing to let her know as soon as she returned so they could pick things back up again. The company would even allow Qing to hold on to her corporate housing, since it seemed unnecessarily bureaucratic to deal with the paperwork when everyone knew she'd be coming back.

It was her first time on an airplane and she could hardly speak the whole time, suffocated under a sensation of terror and resignation that she hadn't experienced before. She gripped the armrests and realized she could, under her feet, feel the friction between the wheels and the tarmac, and then, through her back against the seat, she felt the wind against the wings, and then she felt absolutely nothing as her body got used to the palpation of motion. She was nauseous and thirsty, but she found the flight attendants to be doting in a way that was familiar, respectful, comfortable. She had never been around so many white people in her life and she was glad to have some time to get used to them before she landed. If America was as nice and pretty and polite as these stewardesses and the plane's passengers, that was a good thing. People spoke in soft voices if at all, they waited behind one another to use the bathrooms in which they cleaned up after themselves, and they smiled constantly. They would not bother her, and she felt like she would not bother them. Qing stayed awake the whole time, and it wasn't because she was a chronic insomniac, though she was. It was because she finally understood what it felt like to give herself up to fate—that someone else was in control of her life. A dozen feet away, a pilot would determine whether or not the plane would safely land in

San Francisco for her to make her connecting flight. She was surprised that the thought exhilarated her.

QING KNEW from Chinese newspapers that Lincoln was a famous man and that the city named after him was a famous city, but from what she could tell, this place was no more impressive than the Chinese countryside. The new one-bedroom apartment that Dexin had rented for the two of them (from the description alone, Qing knew she couldn't handle the Little White House) was $190 a month, but she couldn't tell exactly what they were paying for. The apartment buildings—all the buildings in Lincoln, actually—looked like farm factories with tacky red and blue roofs. And there weren't enough of them. The few structures that existed were squat and short, with too much room between them. There were so few people, especially on the street, and the ones she did see looked nothing like Patrick Duffy, the star of Man from Atlantis, an American TV show that had become a phenomenon among young Chinese women. The only things in abundance were cars and space.

When Dexin would drive a few minutes out of the city in their used Mazda 626, Qing would look out the passenger-side window, where all she could see was the flat ground below the sky above, infinities both. There was no road, telephone pole, or person to mar the bigness of yellow earth and pale blue firmament. She was the only person on Earth, a pair of eyeballs that existed between those two planes of soil and heaven, and it was a new consciousness born from a new environment that American TV programs could never prepare her for. China was zhōngguó—*the middle country*—which was a perfectly apt description. It was the middle, the center, and everyone within it was, too. But in America, měiguó—*the beautiful country*—she felt like the land itself was the thing that was beautiful, and everyone and everything existed outside of its margins. Standing on the side of the road with that floating-eyeball vision, she was just a layer between layers. If she tried very hard, she could inhabit that nothingness and forget she had a past or a future, any baggage or responsibilities, a body, weight. *Am I a cloud? If I disappear, who would know?*

Two months after Qing arrived to visit Dexin, it became clear that this trip to America would not be the vacation she had expected. My dad was photographed by *The Lincoln Star* for an article that appeared on the tenth page about local Chinese students who had protested in solidarity with their peers at Tiananmen Square. The students had printed out long ribbon posters on the university's scan-

dot-matrix printers: STOP DEALING WITH BEIJING BUTCHERS, one sign read. PRESIDENT BUSH, SUPPORT DEMOCRACY IN CHINA. Democracy, as far as Dexin understood it, meant making political decisions based on facts instead of greed—a perfectly sensible and not-quite-political position for a highly educated university student like himself to take.

Then came word from Dexin's parents that someone had anonymously informed them of what their son had been up to. The threat was ambiguous, which made the risk clear. It was no longer certain that my father could return home to China safely. When America offered fast-track green cards to Chinese students in response to the June Fourth Incident, my dad jumped at the opportunity. My parents sent for me to come to America, and the three of us found ourselves settling into life as a family in Lincoln, Nebraska.

TWO YEARS after I arrived in the United States, Qing still held out hope that eventually, if enough time passed and the scandal of Dexin's participation in the protests had faded, we could all return to China.

Except that on one early-spring day, it dawned on Qing that she was very, very specifically nauseous. The realization paralyzed her. She waited three months, and her period never came. A friend who, like her, didn't have health insurance told her about a free clinic that Qing could go to. There, a service worker asked her about her situation and whether she had any family or financial support. Qing's English was not good, but her eyes were glossy with tears, and that was an answer unto itself. The woman, with kind confidence, said that she had also been pregnant and also did not have any money, but still made the decision to have the baby. She hadn't regretted it, and would help my mom in any way she could so Qing might not regret it, either. Julia was born in 1991, two years after Qing first arrived in America, while we still lived in that $190 apartment in Lincoln. The four of us slept in the single bedroom—Dexin, Qing, and me on two twin beds, Julia in a hand-me-down crib from Doris.

With Julia's birth, our family had one more child than China's one-child policy allowed for, and Qing's vacation was unquestionably over.

THIS WAS our accidental immigrant story. Geopolitical relations, the whims of politicians, youth activism, and chance opportunities led to one of the biggest waves of modern immigration. Those people—my family included—were later described as part of "America's model minority." But it wasn't clear to anyone, including ourselves, how much of a minority we actually were—a precisely curated subsection of young Chinese people literally picked for their similarities, their obedience, their brains, their pride. These were the golden children of communism, deified and then discarded. My parents and their peers formed the bedrock of the Asian American stereotype that went on to characterize all Asians during the late twentieth century. This group had become a political weapon to disparage other immigrants and American-born minorities for not being cherry-picked for a set of qualities, like we were.

Qing was hardly aware of any of this. All she knew was that she'd been lied to. She had thought that America was where pleasures came from: blue jeans and rock music, Hollywood movies where all the handsome men looked exactly the same, chocolate so precious—half a month's salary for a single bar—that she saved all the wrappers, pressing them in a book like butterflies. But when she finally found herself in America, she found it as comfortless as the countryside labor camps she hated as a child. Up until then, she had been wild, spending irresponsibly, chasing thrills, collecting trinkets. But in the goose chase that defined the early years of her marriage, and the first years of my life, she had taken a wrong turn.

With two children in tow, Qing now had to figure out how to navigate this place in which she'd gotten lost, and find a corner of it that could be something like home.

# ONE

# Road Trippers
## *America*

Before my parents even bought a mattress in Nebraska, they bought a car, a surprisingly cheap thing to acquire, even pre-owned, especially considering what it allowed them to do: come and go on their own terms, without permission or limitations. As long as there was pavement in front of them, they could go wherever they wanted.

This was a novelty. In China, everyone biked and took public transportation. If you were important, you might have a private driver. They had heard that there were places in the United States, too, where people walked and took buses to go to work and shop for food, where non-Chinese people shuffled and squeezed together, breathing in the human smells of people they didn't live with. Those places existed, but they'd likely have to drive there to see them. As my father chased employment between Nebraska, Alabama, and Minnesota, we found ourselves in towns and cities in which cars were the only option to get around, no matter how much or how little money one had. Even to buy a two-dollar gallon of milk, or to check out a free book from the library, a car was a requirement. The only exceptions, as they understood it, were for children who rode yellow school buses.

As their first great purchase, the car became something like a handbook, their first introduction to life as Americans. As a cultural guide, it was surprisingly complete. Obviously it was liberating to own one, and self-deterministic, too—*cars were freedom*, the commercials would remind them. But there was also the everyday extravagance about it, the fact that a car was a necessity and yet demanded so much money to continue to own. All cars, cheap and expensive, used and new, required so much gas to drive and space to accommodate them. The sheer amount of land devoted to parking lots and covered garages was one of the most foreign things about this country.

Then there was the isolation that was required of driving these cars, little protective pods that let you go weeks without experiencing the pedestrian trespass of a stranger's soft hip pressed against your own. For people like my parents whose days out in the world mostly ended when they left school or work, there were few opportunities to see other people simply existing alongside one another—just resting, being, holding on, getting there. It was not infrequent to spend a whole day indoors and inside a car and never get close enough to a stranger to see if their eyes were a color other than brown.

Cars were also dangerous—and this was an important characteristic of all valuable things in America. In the wrong hands, these gifts become weapons. My father would often repeat a horrifying anecdote about a trio of Chinese students he had known in Nebraska who had, just after receiving their licenses, driven to Yellowstone for a vacation. High up in the mountains, rounding the curves of Beartooth Highway, one of these students mistook the gas pedal for the brake and drove them all off a cliff. The first time Dexin took his road test, the DMV examiner told him to pull over and get out. "Sir, you are driving with both feet," he sternly informed my father. "You need to practice doing it the right way before I can score you on this test." *Then why are there two pedals?* my dad wanted to ask. *Someone could get confused. Someone could die. I know some colleagues who did.* Instead, he went home to practice, and redid the test with just his right foot and passed.

This car was the most American thing we owned, and inside it—especially during our own vacations—we were the most American we could possibly be: Dexin, the navigator and optimist, who read the maps and made decisions about which exits we'd take, exclaiming, "This is our home!" to the rest of us as he leaned against the railing of some grand natural vista, or from the top floor of a skyscraper we'd driven hours to see. Qing in the passenger's seat, her feet usually tucked against an Igloo cooler, a garage-sale find, stuffed with cold chicken drumsticks and tea eggs in carefully washed plastic bags from the grocery store. My sister and me in the back, bored and acting our ages. I don't remember ever sitting in a car seat, but I remember my sister in hers, making her way through bags of McDonald's fries as we sped through scenes that changed as slowly as the position of the sun in the sky: fields of soybeans and wheat, pine and hemlock forests, unending universes of greens, yellows, and browns.

Whenever we had a spare day or week to ourselves, we drove. From our home base in Nebraska, we went to Mount Rushmore and the national parks, my dad sweating bullets, his jaw clenched so hard I could see that his head actually looked different from my vantage point in the back seat as we took the switchbacks up and down the ranges with a caravan of impatient drivers behind us. When we lived in Alabama, we'd take day trips to Montgomery and Birmingham to understand what a "downtown" looked like, stopping on county roads for ribs and Wonder Bread. Smokestacks along the way deposited tremendous columns of smoke that did not move, frozen clouds that reached into the sky, wormholes to another world. We drove to the Gulf Coast to wade into the ocean, my dad wearing the skimpy swim trunks that were popular in China during the time he had left, but an aberration among the other men whose swimsuits were more like flags billowing in the wind, giant rectangles of fabric, immodest despite how much they covered. When we took trips out west, I was surprised to see that the most feral parts of nature—patches of furry vegetation alongside streams, the bull's-eye center of hot springs, wildflowers sprouting from the sides of cliff faces—were actually neon-colored, more reflective of the aisles of a toy store than a health-food store: slime green and cough-drop pink, lavender that glowed, electric blues that sizzled.

Beyond these snapshots, I do not remember much about these road trips, mainly because they were boring and all the same through a child's eyes. But preparing for them was exhilarating. Because I got carsick easily, reading wasn't an option, so I'd spend days diligently making mixtapes to listen to during these trips, kneeling on our carpeted floor with my finger on the radio cassette player. I was a Top 40 sharpshooter, smashing the red record button at the exact moment the DJ's voice cut out in order to fill the hour and a half found on both sides of the tape. I mapped out elaborate friendship bracelets to knot and tie during these trips, prechoosing colors and patterns and wrapping them into small bird's nests I'd stash to unwind later in the car, using the big toe of my right foot as an anchor, propped neatly against the back of my dad's headrest, as I braided.

These road trip activities were not exciting in and of themselves. I was not some burgeoning Elsa Peretti or junior DJ Khaled. Rather, these were apparatuses through which I could do the thing that I was actually really, really good at and enjoyed most of all: daydreaming. Free of responsibilities and daily tasks, or even the pressure to play with my sister or talk to my parents, road trips provided me with hours of un-interrupted time to run through my favorite fantasies. What would I buy if I had one hundred dollars? (A haircut at a real salon, new jeans that were actually the size I was when I bought them so they wouldn't be old and gross by the time they actually fit.) What would I change about myself if I could change only five things? (I'd be taller, I'd get rid of the weird callus on the tip of my right thumb, I'd change my hairline, I'd fix my teeth, and I'd be half-Asian—white enough so I'd be pretty, but still Chinese so my parents wouldn't be too disappointed.) And how would it feel to be suddenly popular? (We'd drive into a new city and I would be overwhelmed by a feeling of belongingness, of wholeness, of purpose. While I ate, a group of kids would realize I had Savage Garden play-ing on my tape cassette. *How extremely sophisticated for a sec-ond grader!* they'd think, swarming me.)

I was drawn to the consistency of the landscape; the

repetitive satisfaction of seeing something far away coming closer; the vibration, the hum, the tantric near-stillness you find within constant, gentle motion. Sound itself would bend and warp as I'd get deep into a daydream and realize I was actually just dreaming regularly, having fallen asleep listening to the drone of my parents' soft voices in the front seat, in harmony, but not conversation, with my own voice in my own head.

These daydreams were a way to plot, plan, and psych myself up to manifest what I had imagined. At each rest stop, I purposefully left the car with obsessively considered bait—my Walkman; my favorite journal, which had a lock; a seed-bead necklace I'd made that included a gecko with yellow eyes—and waited for a stranger to pay attention to me, someone to compliment me, to call me *clever, cool, cute,* the best qualities I could picture a person having. They would *get me* in a way that all children dream about being understood, but I took it to desperate levels. From the books I read, I knew that main characters never start out as the obvious hero; I knew that if I encountered the right circumstance, put myself in the way of the exact right person, or opened my eyes up to recognize the adventure within a chore, the opportunity within the challenge, I could finally be the protagonist in my own life.

In actuality, I looked creepy beyond my years, aiming intense eye contact at anyone looking my way, my limbs lolling off banquettes and boulders in postures I thought befitted the covers of a book, myself in repose, a watercolor snapshot of the most dramatic part of the story just before the plot explodes. I look back on photos now and cringe—everyone else with their arms around one another and smiling, and me dramatically grimacing into the distance with one hand shielding my eyes from the sun and the other on my knee, like a pint-sized Christopher Columbus. So desperate to be abducted into a more remarkable life, I made myself essentially unkidnappable.

It wasn't just learning how to pose for vacation pics. There was a lot about how to be a person that I misunderstood from TV and books. Beginning with early-morning lessons in front of the TV in which Elmo and Connie Chung taught me English, my parents relied on entertainment professionals to teach me what they themselves were still learning, subscribing me to every kids' magazine available, going at least once a week (and sometimes every day) to the library, where I'd check out audiobooks and read-along VHS tapes. They enrolled me in a local Head Start program they were told would help low-income families like ours; these lessons were as much for Qing as for me. We learned about good nutrition and healthy emotions—bizarre concepts like cooking with bouillon cubes or counting to ten when you get upset. I found them fascinating in how little they applied to my life and how fun they were to learn about, like I was getting to pass through my own Neighborhood of Make-Believe. It was Miss Linda, a Head Start instructor, who came to Qing and told her in careful, hushed tones that she suspected I knew how to read, a surprising development that she wasn't sure Qing was aware of. But of course Qing knew. She didn't tell Miss Linda about the Chinese characters I used to recognize. Nor did Qing confess our daily ritual, me on her lap, a worn duffel bag next to her feet filled with every book on tape from the children's section, the secondhand boom box reading to us as she flipped the pages with each sound of the chime.

"'What is willpower?' asked Toad," spoke the narrator.

"What is willpower?" Qing and I would repeat, training our voices to go up at the end, which let Americans know that a sentence was a question.

It made sense that I was retaining more than just spoken English. But a four-year-old who could read, Miss Linda tried to impress upon Qing, was gifted and talented, and not a problem child like everyone had been treating me.

Up until that point, I was a daycare delinquent, and I was bad in an impressively diverse set of ways. I wasn't just a biter, or a worm eater, or a revenge pooper, or a rule breaker, or a runaway, or a destroyer, or a puppy dog—a creature I had never seen in real life but was fond of on TV—who demanded to take all her meals off the floor. I was all of these things every single day.

Time-out was a daily occurrence. Qing later told me that I was so proud of being singled out for the honor of being the only one—every day!—to enjoy quiet time in a corner that she thought time-out was some kind of merit for outstanding students. And it was: I was outstanding at being bad. "I had time-out today and I didn't cry," I recall telling Qing when she'd come by to fetch me, wearing new pants and carrying my old, soiled ones in a plastic bag. She'd gaze upon my face, covered in colorful painted polka dots and a huge grin, with dried mud under my nails. She remembered what it was like at the daycare she was expelled from and how miserable she had been. She was proud that I was doing things she had never done and seemed to be enjoying them. "Wǒde mā ya!" she'd respond. *You are my special and strong girl.* Hǎo háizi."

But after I found books, my frenetic energy was refocused, and I began to understand that there was a "right" way and a "wrong" way to do things, and your natural preference for either option depended on whether you were good and hardworking or bad and lazy, and that was fundamental to whether people liked you or ignored you. Learning how to read exposed me to *Goofus and Gallant* and other etiquette guides that revealed that I had misunderstood what "being good" was all about. Feeling ashamed instead of proud about time-out was the end of me being in time-out.

Nevertheless, books were hardly sufficient in clearing

everything up. It wasn't just that American punishments seemed like rewards (imagine being sent to your room and complaining about it—imagine having your own room!). Or that tough American lessons seemed to miss the point—like the idea of willpower, for example, which suggested that I had the option to ask for more than one cookie in the first place. It was also the truism that main characters are just misunderstood heroes, and that the key to belonging is finding people with whom you share the same opinions and hobbies. It was also that it was okay to get yelled at by your parents (every hero gets yelled at right before they run away and become heroes), but if they yelled at each other, that meant they were going to get divorced.

Even though I stopped getting in trouble at school, home was a different story. I was constantly infuriating Qing. Unlike my father, who reserved his emotional outbursts for poor service or disrespectful strangers, she kept her anger for her loved ones. Yelling was a rarity, but her wrath was constant, and was usually triggered by casual asides that demeaned her efforts to protect us. On road trips, in our family pod on wheels, my parents' complementary anger ensured that someone was mad at all times. Dexin spoke slowly, in deliberately simple English meant to make anyone on the receiving end of it—dispassionate motel attendants, teenage clerks, bored ticket collectors—feel about as worthwhile as a used Kleenex. It would end at the threshold of the car, however, as

Qing's rage took over, and I was usually the reason why: I had said I was happy I didn't have to practice piano during vacation; I had mentioned I hadn't packed any books except for "fun" ones; I had hit my sister because she unwound the spool of my favorite cassette; I had not only had the gall to ask for a toy from the gift shop, but deliberately wanted something expensive with no educational value. Her anger poured out in Chinese, of which I could really only understand two-thirds, and I could only respond in Chinese as sophisticated as that of a baby's: "*That's not right! You are not right*," I'd wail, too ashamed to explain myself in English, another admission of a way I had disappointed everyone. And, besides, Qing wouldn't be able to understand, either. Having learned English from textbooks, Qing could read and write English far better than I could, but speaking-wise, she was as bad at English as I was bad at Chinese.

During good conversations, we both self-censored and modulated to each other's comprehension, speaking in carefully honed Chinglish that relied on the more elementary vocabulary of our own stronger language. Decades later, as I watched my husband talk to his mother about the female naturalist Margaret Mead, I listened to their conversation grow existential, then political, and then sentimental, and I couldn't unstick myself from the first part—couldn't fathom how I would even describe the word *naturalist* in Chinese, when I didn't even know the word for *nature*.

The conversations we could have had should haunt me. But they don't, because how can I miss something I never had? I don't remember it being any other way. One of my earliest memories—the kind you force yourself to remember because the experience is so disorienting that you feel yourself growing up while it's happening—was a talking-to. The circumstances in which I had gotten in trouble are lost to me now, but Qing was attempting to explain the concept of being considerate. It was important that I know what this word meant, she said solemnly, in a voice that made me feel like I also needed to be as mature as possible.

"*Do you know the word for* respect *in English?*" she asked in Mandarin. "*You need to be more respectful. Do you know the word for* respect?"

I nodded my head. I was pretty sure I knew. On TV, there was only one word people had to whisper when they said it, and they said it only around grown-ups, with the same searching, grave countenance of my mother's.

"Sexy," my four-year-old self said. "I need to be sexy."

Neither of us said anything further as we both realized we had missed by miles, and that miles was the best either of us could hope for.

When Qing was angry, it all fell apart. Expressing myself in the most elementary of ways—to my mother, about something that had happened, about something I was feeling—was inordinately difficult, nearly impossible, and unwelcome. Unfortunately, failing to express myself was an infraction of one of her big rules, too. Another first memory was when I got in trouble for failing to be called on to recite a poem during a parent showcase for Saturday Chinese school because I didn't raise my hand high enough. "No matter what you think. No matter what you say. If people do not hear you and understand you, you did nothing. *You understand?* Nǐ míngbái ma?" Eventually, when it came to Qing, I stopped trying to explain, to express. It was easier just to shut up and say sorry, to silently sob over the injustice until I fell asleep. In the car, I'd lie down with my face tucked into the crevice where the seat back met the seat bottom and press the top of my head against the car door, the seat belt pulled out loose to the point where it'd stop retracting. The staccato vibration from the road would be perfectly in tune with the one emanating from my overoxygenated brain. Sleeping after crying jags was my favorite way to sleep. I was powerless to it, merely a passenger. The peace I felt was absolute.

THERE WAS ONE road trip we took that turned out not to be a road trip at all. I had just turned seven, my three-year-old sister just out of diapers and baby talking with a heavy Alabamian drawl. Everything we owned was carefully placed inside a U-Haul trailer hitched to the back of our car. We drove without stopping much (we did not stop much to begin with, in general, on our road trips), and I remember that Dad did not use the map as much as he normally did. We got to a motel and we unpacked a rice cooker, and I thought that was so fun, that we were cooking in the same room we were sleeping in, which was almost like how Laura Ingalls Wilder did it living on the prairie with her pioneer family. I didn't like to talk about those books at school—they were boring, the other kids told me, and I didn't disagree. But my life was boring, and reading Laura talk about the pride she had in owning only a few things, and taking care of them well, made me feel proud of the few things we had, and also took care of well. During a Scholastic Book Fair at school, I persuaded Qing to buy me the boxed paperback set of the Little House series so I could read and reread my favorite two books without having to re-check them out of the library every week: the one where Laura moved with her family to Plum Creek and made enemies with the rich girl Nellie Oleson, and *Farmer Boy*, from which I read and reread the specific passages describing the outlandish things that Almanzo and his family ate for meals—twisted doughnuts and stacked pancakes, sweet baked beans and yellow cheese. I read them as Qing made dinner in the rice cooker with eggs she scrambled in the almost-done rice, mixed with torn-up bits of Carl Buddig ham that came in envelopes the size of garden seed packets and cost far less. Dexin emerged from the bathroom wearing a suit, something I'd never seen him in before. I stared at him.

"Well, I'm going to work tomorrow," he told us.

I waited, listening.

"This is our home," he said. "We're Minnesotans now."

I couldn't believe it. "Are we in Plum Creek?" I ventured.

"Puh-lum shénme? No. This is Shakopee," he said, scooping my sister up in his too-big suit in cheap, shiny fabric that gave him the effect of a man who was headed to sleep, not work. "But we might move closer to where my new bàngōngshì is, in Eden Prairie."

I couldn't speak. A prairie. In Minnesota. In *Eden*. Laura had described the prairie in magical terms—a vast place of soft light and golden grass. *And on the whole enormous prairie there was no sign that any other human being had ever been there.* That was where we were going. It was a miracle I had dreamed true.

TWO

# Homecomers
## *China Part 1*

I say this with the maximum amount of love a person
can have for a place they have no interest in ever living
in again, but, to me, the most remarkable thing about
the place where I grew up is how exceptionally unremark-
able it is. A colleague once told me she had heard of a place
in the Midwest where food chains go to test out new concepts. Apparently, she told me, it's because the residents
comprise the exact average of American appetites, the cap-
italistic definition of neutral.* In Eden Prairie, one gets the
sense that there is exactly the right number of grocery
stores, gas stations, and parks for the number of people

---

*It turned out the place was Columbus, Ohio—a veritable metropolis compared to
our Minnesota suburb.

who live there. Plus, Dexin's office was there, and so we built our home there.

We constructed our first house from the ground up, which was objectively an extravagance, but developers had flooded Eden Prairie, making it not much more expensive to buy a customizable starter home than an existing one that came with its own history and ghosts. Qing had lived only in apartments her entire life, and she fantasized about what it'd be like to completely control the cleanliness of the entirety of her home, including what happened on the other side of the walls, and even within the walls (the real danger with apartments, condos, and townhouses, as she maintains to this day, is that you may be unlucky enough to end up with a filthy neighbor who attracts rats and snakes to live in the insulation).

The house took half a year to build, and I found it all to be endlessly entertaining. While Qing and Dexin worked with designers to choose simple linoleum with tiny rosebuds for the kitchen, and a tasteful oak trim to match the kitchen cabinets, my sister and I would "play house" in the model homes, pretending to watch TV on prop sets made of thin plastic, talking to our fake crushes on our fake cordless phones, arms and legs splayed, shoes on the beds.

My parents considered which exterior style was the most "us." Were we Colonial or Craftsman? Perhaps we were Tudor. Maybe Tuscan? Qing did not care if these words had historical context. To her, they were like the flavors of salad dressing, like French or ranch. But even if it's intellectually odd to see a home built in the style of eighteenth-century New England situated right next to another one inspired by Italian wine country, the neighborhood homeowners association flattened all differences with a combination of imperious edicts. They lopped off anything that stuck out, from quirky landscaping to exterior paint colors that deviated too far from beige. Our siding was the color of nondairy creamer; the home to the right of ours was one shade warmer, like the pages of a decades-old paperback, and the home to the left of it was one shade grayer, like the inside of a carton of expensive eggs. Qing picked out a giant boulder from a rock quarry to place in the front yard (we were the only ones in our neighborhood with one), and we planted the sod ourselves, giant jelly rolls of grass that I helped my dad spread out across our front and back lawns so that they eventually touched our neighbors'. No one had fences, and so, when looking out from our backyard deck, it almost felt like we were idling in some sort of formation, each of our homes' rears backed up against one another's, like a gauntlet turned inside out, standing guard on the banks of a wide, green river.

After the initial up-front effort, the home stayed pretty much the same throughout my childhood and adulthood, and even today, when I go home to visit, nearly everything is as I remember it. The trapped-in-amber quality is because of my father, for whom spending only the minimum viable amount of money on items that will last forever is something like religion. The reason that the home is still inhabitable and pleasant is because of Qing, who is devoted to protecting it from dust, clutter, crud, and age.

"Mom is not *oh-see-dee*," she told us much later. She had learned the word for obsessive compulsive disorder from my sister, who was doing a medical rotation in the psychiatric wing of a hospital and told Qing that one quality of OCD was that carrying out these compulsions provided temporary relief, but not happiness. "For me, I am so happy to clean," Qing has said. On her hands and knees, Qing will wipe the honey-blond floors a few times a day and pick long strands of our black hair out of the carpet. It was a happy coincidence that she adored cleaning, an affinity that came after her love of being in clean spaces, which was a luxury that her mother—my laolao—provided, keeping Qing's childhood home in exacting, fastidious order. Laolao had and has, we suspect, actual OCD. When Qing was growing up, Laolao would remake all the beds if she noticed that someone had sat on one of them during the day. She would also force Qing and her sister to take full baths before getting into bed every night, an incredible proposition given that, at the time, there was no running water inside their home, and the state issued only a single bathing ticket per person a week to access the community plumbing at the center of their housing district.

Laolao approached everything with the principles of good hygiene, long health, and predictability. Despite this, disorder, disease, and disaster still determined the major redirections of her life. Her childhood was dotted with ill health and long spells of sickness, and when she was in her early thirties, a local doctor took a look at the coloration around her lips and told her that there was something wrong with her ovaries. A subsequent hysterectomy found that the doctor was right—there was a mass of hair and teeth in one of the ovaries that was the source of her pain. Afterward, Laolao began to put on weight, ballooning from just under 80 pounds to well over 180, a point of pride during a time when there was not enough to eat. But, as time went on, the weight remained, and her fatness became another unforeseen misfortune she was compelled to repeat like a campfire ghost story.

These random turns of fate made Laolao paranoid and underscored much of her relationship with Qing, who did not seem to understand that life is brutal and unfair, and that protecting yourself against it requires daily vigilance and hand-wringing. Whenever I'd ask Qing about what Laolao had done when Qing misbehaved, my mom didn't have much of an answer. "She get sick easy" was always her response.

The children of handwringers do not immediately become handwringers themselves. That comes later, when they venture out of the hygienic circle polished by their mothers. But within the circle, life feels as safe and predictable as the homes in Eden Prairie. My life, growing up, was one of comfort and rules, and so I spent most of my energy searching for some "uniqueness" within the palette of beige.

That word, *unique*, was loaded—especially in Eden Prairie—a compliment as much as a warning.

"What a unique dessert," a teacher would say about the red-bean paste I had brought in for a classroom ice cream sundae party before she threw it in the trash.

"You've got such a unique life!" my neighbor whose children I babysat would respond when I told her I wasn't sure how she wanted me to bathe the kids—should I let them bring in toys, and should I use bubble bath, and if so, how? I only remembered taking showers with my mom and my little sister, and it certainly wasn't playtime.

"Your friends sound so unique," a friend's mom remarked when I came home from college during Thanksgiving my freshman year and mentioned that a group of us in the coed dorm had attended a midnight drag show.

My struggle for suitable uniqueness took on a variety of embarrassing forms. There was the time I decided to secretly write *hi* all over the walls and posters in my fourth-grade classroom. I imagined that I'd gradually arouse the curiosity and admiration of the whole grade, leading up to some culmination during which I'd finally reveal that I was the mastermind behind it all, except I drew on a picture my best friend, Kate, had made (a kind gesture, in my eyes, since I was inviting her into the center of this mystery), and she cried when she saw it, and then I also cried, and everyone knew it was me and there was nothing mysterious about any of it, just weird. There was the time when I saved all my babysitting money from the summer to buy a heap of drugstore makeup before school started that fall, Cover-Girl Lipslicks the shade of a twenty-four-hour scab, loose glitter in a plastic pot that'd get everywhere as I dabbed it onto my cheeks on the school bus. I arrived to class every day with makeup that gave the effect that I had lived a very difficult life of glamour and ruin, except I was also ten. There was the time I insisted on re-creating the complicated hairstyles I saw in fashion catalogs each day before fifth grade, carving zigzag parts into my hair that only accentuated the expansive Larry King hairline I had, securing anemic braids the thickness of bucatini onto my scalp with plastic butterfly clips. Qing had always cut my hair herself. When I was lucky and she had time, that meant a shoulder-length hairstyle that attracted neither compliments nor looks of pity; when I was unlucky and she was rushed, that meant my hair was gathered in a ponytail that she would lop the ends off of in one flat slice, so I could never wear it loose and down and pretty until the next haircut, for which I prayed I got lucky. I got lucky a lot in fifth grade, which was nice.

These attempts kept me occupied, but they did not work, in the sense that I did not appear to be more charming. After I spent a weekend undoing the hems of my too-short jeans, which added an inch of chewed-up denim in undulating layers of indigo and grime, my friend Maggie gently broke the news that she had gotten an invitation to sit with the popular girls at lunch, and she knew I'd understand that that was a big deal for someone like us, and she hoped it'd happen to me sometime soon. It was like being in a movie, I thought, which made me feel somewhat better.

I blamed it on my glasses, my teeth, my twiggy frame, my last name. But most of all, I blamed it on my hairline. It was my father's hairline, which might suit an old man like him, but on a kid like me, I knew it was disturbing. It was shaped like a receding hairline, but it had not receded from anything; I was born with it curving like a cul-de-sac and blurry around all the edges, but especially on the areas that carved inward above each temple, sprouting frizzy, thin baby hairs like little puffs of smog. The only other person in my entire school with this hairline was my fifth-grade teacher, Mr. Ross, who was everyone's favorite despite looking like the groundskeeper of a very haunted mansion. I worked hard to draw attention away from my hairline with elaborate hairstyles and headbands, which only had the opposite effect. At some point, I decided I'd be better off hiding it instead, carefully wetting a hairbrush in the sink and combing my hair into valances across my temples; as it dried, the whole effect would come undone, and so I found ways to wet it throughout the day, which helped neither my appearance nor my social clout.

Fixing my hairline was my number-one hobby when my parents let me know we were finally going to make a trip to China. It had been a decade since Qing had boarded that flight to Lincoln, and she wouldn't have risked trying to return any earlier. She had heard of other friends of theirs who attempted to visit home. Some were stopped at the airport in Beijing and interrogated. One man, upon returning to the States, recounted how he had been followed by strange men as soon as he arrived, who shadowed him during his entire time in China and did not even attempt to hide what they were doing. Qing's parents, my laoye and laolao, applied for visas to come and live with us for as long as the government would allow, a maximum of one year. And though they were both ultimately successful, it was an inordinately difficult process—a fact they were reminded of throughout (*It could have been easier, more convenient, with fewer hassles*, they were told—*but only if . . .* ). My father's parents' visa applications were denied twice in succession.

They stopped trying. All this had chilled my parents to the idea of returning. But after ten years, more of their friends had made the trip without incident. Dexin was making better money, and Qing had started working as an accountant, organizing numbers—instead of words—into sense. They began planning, and so did I.

I WAS EXCITED by the trip. Finally! A time to feel superior and cosmopolitan in front of my yokel cousins still trapped in what my teachers had always described—with a sympathetic look in my direction—as "a *third world* country." Now that I was in sixth grade, my entire comprehension of social dynamics was formed through comparing myself to others: There were the other Asian girls in my classes, including Meng, who also went to Chinese school and whose hair was bouncy and glossy like Monica's from *Friends*, and who loved anime. There were Jodie and Liz, who had cute freckles, real Abercrombie jeans, and wore their hair gelled back in high and tight ponytails because their hairlines were gorgeous. But they were Korean and adopted, so the comparisons ended there. Then there was my sister, who was gregarious and cute, and I hated her for it—I made her open the front door whenever strangers knocked and pick up the phone when I didn't recognize the number on the caller ID, even though I was four years older. And further from my circle were all the other kids in the surrounding school districts who attended Chinese school on Saturdays, nearly all of whom spoke Mandarin more fluently than I did. But I was definitely not as weird as them, these child geniuses far more brilliant and demented than myself, including a twelve-year-old boy who constructed an entire laptop computer from salvaged parts that he then brought with him to class in order to watch porn during vocabulary lessons.

There was also my best group of friends—Rori, Samira, Juls, and Kelsey—to whom I never really compared myself, and I never questioned why. They loved books as much as I did, and we spent our time talking about what we read and listened to, and attempting to write a book together for which Oprah would invite us onto her show as the youngest authors who ever lived (I believe Rori still has the original manuscript of *Time of Day* in her family's garage). I say with some certainty now as an adult that these first authentic friendships changed everything for me. But at the time, those friendships were just there—comfortable, uncomplicated, undramatic, easy—and thus not interesting enough to torture myself over. I felt I had nothing to prove to them, not realizing that was something rare and thus worthy of cherishing, and placed the entirety of my social energy elsewhere.

For this trip to China, I had much to prove. And so I

would wear my coolest clothes, the ones that revealed the exact right amount of midriff (a handspan) between the bottom hem of my double-layered spaghetti-strap tops and the waistband of my low-rise cargo pants. I would not be like my mom, whose clothes were both aggressively plain and kind of ugly, too—too-big T-shirts with foreign cartoon characters and unfashionable blue jeans from brands no one had heard of. I would also bring my Discman and a sleeve of burned CD-Rs, because I suspected and hoped that I'd be bored by what we would be doing, but also looked forward to getting the chance to show them off—certainly they didn't have things like music in China. I placed everything in layers in my backpack, bringing everything of value I owned. Over the course of a month, Qing also filled the open and empty suitcases that had been sitting cavernous in her bedroom, lining the edges with the same washing-machine-faded clothes that had become her uniform for ten years to cushion the real cargo inside: jumbo bottles of vitamins from Sam's Club, sticks of deodorant and tubes of toothpaste, generously cut pants and blouses from Dressbarn for my laolao, who was an average size in the Midwest but too big to shop for in China. There were blood pressure monitors, hearing aids for my dad's father, my yeye, a leather belt for my uncle, and lightweight quilted jackets and vests for my aunts and cousins.

I surveyed the suitcases Qing filled as we neared the date, satisfied that these were things I had no desire for.

The plane trip would be the first flight I would remember. More important, I was traveling the farthest out of anyone in my class—farther than Cabo San Lucas or Playa del Carmen. Farther even than the Bahamas (wherever that was). But telling people I was going to China seemed to deflate conversation, not enliven it. No one had gone before, there was no handy advice to administer, it seemed like a family affair; *sounds like a good time—have fun!* We'd be traveling for a full day, which seemed like an eternity to be in such a state of rapture, and I was prepared. I had magazines and books, my music, a magnetic five-in-one travel game set I had negotiated the purchase of, and more embroidery floss for bracelets. The quick flight to San Francisco was exciting, and nearly exactly what I had imagined flying to be like: ceremonious and cinematic. I looked out the porthole window and imagined that I had a movie camera over my left shoulder, and I tried to think tender thoughts and make myself cry. But boarding the China Eastern flight in California was different. Firstly, I was surrounded by other Chinese families, but they were not like my parents' friends, the ones who sent their kids to Chinese school. I couldn't understand many of them; they spoke loudly in dialects I wasn't even sure were Chinese. Many were traveling with elders, which was exotic in and of itself. The Chinese families I knew were other orphan families like mine whose grandparents were visitors and spent the majority of the time keeping to themselves lest they attract any American attention. These grandparents, as far as I could tell, were not visiting, and they didn't want or care to be invisible. Rather, they did whatever they wanted, spitting watermelon seeds directly onto the airplane carpet, lying on the pass-throughs to sleep, ignoring the dings of the seat belt re-minder as well as the Chinese flight attendants who tried to get them back into their seats. These were Chinese people behaving like they didn't care what other people thought of them, something I had never seen before, and I felt some-thing sharp unglue inside me. I closed my eyes, lulled by the vacuum noise of the plane. When I opened them again, it was somehow the next day, and we were about to land. I had missed my chance to daydream, plot, and manifest. Nothing good could come next.

Qing's sister and her husband met us at the airport. Qing embraced Li Bai and cried. I did not hug anyone be-cause no one hugged me, and it was excruciatingly awk-ward to realize I could not say any of the things in Mandarin that I thought one was supposed to say during homecom-ings like these—"I'm so happy to be home," "You haven't changed at all!"—both because I didn't know the words, but also because they were not the truth. Our luggage was swept up by the adults, and I scrambled to help so I wouldn't have to say anything, and then we were on our way, in a van driving alongside a freeway that looked like what freeways look like. But the sky we drove underneath was unlike anything I had seen before; it was the same color as our home, a beige-yellow-gray, the sun a suggestion of light, a color—almost red—instead of luminescence itself.

China was nothing like what I had anticipated. Jinan was bigger than any city I had ever been in, and dirtier, too, which scared me since I only knew Chinese people to be neat freaks. And though the insides of my relatives' apartments were spotless, I was astonished by the things they had—decorative urns taller than my father on his tiptoes, marble floors I could almost see my reflection in, fancy televisions that were larger and flatter than anything I had seen inside my friends' homes. "Are they rich?" I asked Qing, who shrugged. "So are we poor?" She glared at me.

I stayed mostly mute as my parents made the rounds visiting friends and old coworkers, hoping that I could use my silence to my advantage to appear more mysterious, or even sophisticated. We drove through my dad's hometown, where I was shocked to see many girls my age sporting the same dramatic hairline as mine, their hair pulled back, the bald corners of their forehead on full display. *Don't they know they look ridiculous?* I thought. I pressed my own forehead against the car window in case one of them glanced my way and might be instantly edified at the sight of my carefully combed hair.

We went out to restaurants the size of department stores, and ate in individual rooms around massive circular tables that could seat twenty with lazy Susans the circumference of Hula-Hoops. There were lots of people who wanted to treat my parents to dinner, and it felt strange to see my parents as social, popular people, though they absolutely did not behave like they were popular—they were still unsure and, at some points, even seemed cowed by it all. "*What happened to you, Qing?*" her friends would gibe. "*Trying to appear modest for us?*" She'd smile and blink in the same way she would during my parent-teacher conferences.

Meals frequently started with sea cucumber, spiky and soft like the waterlogged finger of a demon warlord. My laoye had brought dehydrated sea cucumbers to America when he came to stay, and they were nutritious and expensive—like medicine, he said—and so I learned to take them like medicine, using chopsticks to place the bitter pill-sized chunks at the back of my throat to swallow without tasting or chewing. In China, this technique was met with amusement. "*You don't know how to recognize good things!*" adults would laugh.

My silence, too, didn't come across as enigmatic, but rather as strange and doltish. I didn't know how to answer the question "*What's it like in America?*" How could I explain?

It was boring. Maybe it was less dusty? China seemed like one gigantic, sprawling city, which meant the America I knew was basically the countryside. School was easy. Chinese school was hard. I settled on saying, *"The sky is blue,"* which seemed effective since it at least elicited a smile from everyone.

One afternoon, my aunt told me and Julia that we'd be visiting the middle school my mom's best friend Li Yu's son, Bin Bin, attended. We wouldn't have to say anything if we didn't want to, she quickly offered, as she saw the corners of my lips pinch. And besides, all the kids have been taking English classes for years, and it'd be good practice for them! I had seen Bin Bin leave for school wearing a uniform I thought looked ridiculous—a white-and-blue tracksuit that made him look like a soccer coach. And so I wore my best spaghetti-strap combination and cargo shorts, psyched myself up to be adored, and headed to school with him and my sister in tow.

Bin Bin held my hand as we entered the gates, which embarrassed me since it was the first time a boy had held my hand. But my self-consciousness soon took on another form. I immediately understood that however dull and unimpressive I was in Minnesota, I was exponentially so here. *"What's wrong with her?"* a boy shouted at Bin Bin, excited about a potential confrontation. *"She's from America,"* he responded, gripping my hand. Inside, Julia and I sat on the side of the classroom, watching the English lesson unfold as students stood up when called upon. The writing on the chalkboard was familiar, the same kind of gently sloped letters with tight little tails that I recognized was the same as my mom's, and I realized that hers was learned and trained into her, as unique as a mass-produced snowflake ornament.

And then, all of a sudden, we were at the front of the class, and the questions began—"What is your favorite berry?" "What do you do for fun?" "Do you like Michael Jordan?" Those were easy, but they made me feel like I was a baby, or that the other students were babies. "What do you think about the president of the United States?" "What do you think about our English?" And then, "What do you think about the United States bombing the Chinese embassy in—zěnme shuō?—Bèi'ěrgéláidé?"

I blinked at the last question. "Excuse me, what?"

"*Bèi. Ěr. Gé. Lái. Dé. Nán. Sī. Lā. Fū,*" the student enunciated, and then turned her attention to the teacher. "*It only happened a few months ago, how could she not know what I'm talking about?*" she spit in Mandarin.

"Yu-go-su-la-vi-ah," the teacher translated fruitlessly.

I still had no clue. Was she saying Yugoslavia? Belgrade? The only thing that sounded anything like Belgrade, to me, was Belgravia, and that was from Sherlock Holmes, which made me more confused. "If people want to know anything about America . . ." I said, failing. Julia sensed that the attention had turned, and she slithered with her back to the wall, back to the seats we had been sitting on. The decorum had broken, and the students started talking and laughing with one another, maybe at me, even, and I was ashamed that I couldn't even tell. The teacher barked for attention, and just as suddenly, the class gelled back into order—the hierarchies once again restored.

THE ONLY PERSON in China I never felt like I had to perform in front of was my laolao, who was the nearest proximal thing that I had ever encountered to a fairy godmother. She looked the part: She was short and round, the shape of a plucked Cornish hen. I had spent time with her before— she had stayed with us for a year when I was six, when we lived in Alabama. In the swampy American heat, she was perpetually overheated and damp, so she wore very little, always mopping the sweat from underneath the folds of her breasts against her belly, her waistline against her upper thighs, her jowls against her neck. My naked, sweaty grandma had a face that wasn't unlike the illustrations of Toad from *Adventures of Frog and Toad*, a children's book of morality tales in which Toad, perpetually ornery and self-ish, is the comic foil to Frog, who is tall and green and cheerful and responsible. Laolao's face was also wider than it was long, and her frown and worry lines still ticked up mischievously at the edges, scowling and snickering all at once.

Back in Alabama, my laolao told me she could do magic. I would try to learn by doing morning exercises with her in the courtyard of our apartment complex, using the knuckles on my pointer fingers to rhythmically knead my temples, my eye sockets, and the hard bone underneath my upper lip in circular motions, and watching her pillowy arms push and pull the air as she did tai chi. *"There's a ball of qì I've got here, and I can push you over with it if I wanted to,"* she would tease in Mandarin, and I'd beg her to show me. *"I said if I wanted to! And I don't want to."* And then she'd laugh like a villain. I loved it.

I didn't have many friends in Alabama, but I wasn't embarrassed to bring the friends I did have around to see Laolao. "She's weird, yes, but it's because she can do magic," I'd brag. "She told me she knows how to live to be two hundred years old, and she'll tell you the secret, too, once she thinks you can handle it. She could feel your belly and know exactly what you ate that day!" These friends would stare at her with suspicion and awe, and Laolao would ask me if my friends were slow or something. *"They're looking at you like that because I told them that you can kill them with qì."*

"Xiǎo huàidàn!" she'd joke in pretend horror. *You bastard! You little bad egg!*

She loved America for how easy it was to find cheap clothing in sizes that fit her and for its prevalence of garage sales, and learned only enough English to navigate those two scenarios ("How much?" "Too much." "*One* dollar."). She kept my secrets when I told my mother I had practiced an hour of piano, but had only played the same Czerny scales over and over as I read a book instead. She saw the clothes my sister and I wore, and decided she'd make us ones that were special, using garage-sale sewing patterns and old sheets and XXL muumuus, and I didn't complain when I wore them, because I loved her, though they made me look like a scrap-fabric version of JonBenét Ramsey. She made us quilts that I adored, and for a long time, I couldn't sleep unless I had Laolao's brown blanket on top of me in the exact right way, one graying corner tucked into the right side of my mouth, tasting like how she smelled, like sweaty bread, something earthy, and a little like medicine.

Her apartment in China also smelled just like her, like a witch's lair, and it was filled with ephemera that she had clipped and saved as proof to be used later, small talismans from newspapers and pamphlets advertising self-massage techniques and daily health rituals, jars of dried herbs and packets of pills, all of which promised a longer life. I was surprised to see how messy it was, and some parts of the home were legitimately dirty, and I wondered how Qing could stand it. Laolao used to be obsessive about cleanliness,

Qing had explained, but after she had surgery, she lost that drive, her OCD excised along with the removal of the hairy teratoma. With a perverse sense of pride, I noticed that Laolao's apartment was smaller than our home in America, though I felt guilty about who I was prideful against.

THE REST of the trip was a series of minor humiliations. I dialed in to the internet on my uncle's home computer and typed "tiananmen square" into the AOL search engine, curious about the firewall I had heard about in school, and then "tiananmen square protests" and then "tiananmen square massacre" when I couldn't find anything I was looking for, pleased that I would get to tell everyone this rumor was true. I'm not sure what exactly happened next, but something definitely did, and my uncle came home from his government job the next day and told me I wasn't allowed to use his computer anymore. My extended family members seemed not at all interested in my life in America, and the only comfort I had from not being asked questions was that I knew I couldn't answer them. At the home of one of my parents' friends, following an elaborate dinner out where I ordered a dish just for myself to be bratty, I sat in a room with their son, awkward and puny with huge glasses, with teeth that looked like they had been cut out with safety scissors, and I was mean to him. Throwing a belt at his head in response to something snarky he said, I laughed when he failed to catch it, but fell silent when I realized that the jade buckle had smacked him in the face, and he started to cry and ran out of the room with blood trickling from his mouth. We left immediately, Qing grabbing me by the wrist with a brutality that scared me, and I cried during the entire car ride back to my aunt's home, where we were staying. Right before we arrived, I felt the combustion in my head migrate down my body, into my guts, and then out of my pants. In the bathroom, naked and sobbing, I stood in the dark as Qing hosed the diarrhea off me in angry, loud silence. Even still, before bed, she massaged my hands, as my fingers had a tendency to overextend and freeze that way whenever I'd hyperventilate.

The next day, I didn't want to get out from beneath the quilt. Whatever food poisoning I had gotten hadn't completely evacuated from my body, and so I opted to stay with Laolao while the rest of the family went out to do errands. We would be leaving the day after next, and there was some last-minute shopping to do, but there was nothing I needed, and certainly nothing I wanted. Sitting on the couch, my stomach would gurgle, and Laolao would fart, and we'd look at each other occasionally and make faces.

She had not changed much since we had said goodbye to her in Alabama, though her hair was grayer and she now was walking with a slight limp. She was still fat and soft, and I took every excuse I could get to push up against her even though she said being that close made her too hot and to get off. But I couldn't resist. Her body was like a handful of steamed egg custard, silky and springy, wet and cool on the surface but with a tenacious heat below, like she had just been sitting on the counter cooling all afternoon after spending hours in the oven braising.

In her apartment, she read the paper and I read my book, and I felt almost okay. I caught her at one point applying the deodorant we had brought from America onto her forehead, and I told her it was only for her armpits, but she said, "*Who said? Americans don't know anything. I sweat more on my face.*" I was sweating, too, still clammy from food poisoning, and she let me put some deodorant on my forehead. Eventually she went into her room to nap, and I was all alone; the only noise punctuating the silence of the afternoon was the brass horn in my belly. I went to the bathroom, locking the door behind me, in case Laolao forgot I was there and walked in.

I hadn't eaten much since the night before, but there was enough that I had something to flush. The bathroom was unpleasant, dank, and dim, like the public toilets at national parks, with cement walls and tile floors, and mildew in every right angle. I hurried to wash my hands to escape from the room, fearing what I might see if I looked.

Except when I went to turn the doorknob, the handle would not budge. Kneeling on the floor, blinking in the dimness of the room, I realized that the rusted lock button had gotten stuck, and with a rapidly blossoming panic, I tried to pick at it with one finger, and then with a hairpin I had found, and then I just tried to force the knob to move in a—in any—direction, and it still would not. I returned to the toilet, the anxiety of the situation reawakening my guts.

"LAOLAO," I whisper-screamed, not wanting to alert anyone else in the courtyard to my situation through the open window. But I knew it was futile. Even if she had literally been in the bathroom with me, her sleep was so deep it was impossible to wake her. I was so thirsty, but I knew I could not drink the water from the sink. The air was thick and hot, the sweet and bilious reek of diarrhea nearly visible as cartoon stink lines in my delirium. I turned on the faucet, thinking that the flowing water might do something purifying, and continued to perform my Sisyphean tasks, shuffling from the doorknob to the toilet. Eventually, I gave up and sat on the toilet with my upper half folded over my thighs, my head resting on my crossed arms, waiting for death or my family to return.

It was some time before they came home. My uncle found a drawerful of keys and worked through them as I sat-lay there, not really moving, too spent to pay attention to my own rescue. The commotion grew louder while becoming more muted, as I drifted in and out, suffocating on my own fumes. I don't remember exactly what happened or how long it took, but eventually the door swung open with violence. I lifted my head up and saw an old man and a kid, presumably a locksmith with his apprentice, looking awfully pleased with themselves, and I quickly lowered my head again because I didn't want to see their expressions change. The only thing that cut through the buzzing in my ears was Laolao's phlegmy cackle.

# THREE

# Time Sharers
## *Resorts*

One day during my last year of high school, Qing and Dexin did something unprecedented. They went to our local mall to walk in laps for exercise, stopped at one of the kiosks that was situated between a seller hawking synthetic ponytail extensions and another selling fleece pajamas that could be folded into pillows, and spent $50,000 on "points" in a global time-share program that promised them a lifetime of vacations that would eventually, they were assured, pay for itself.

When they came home, they showed us the official faux-leather brochure that was filled with images of beaches, serene hotel lobbies, and daiquiris the color of nail polish. My sister and I were skeptical. Until then, we had never gone on a vacation like this, but we had some idea of what to expect. Our classmates had gone, and we knew of the experiences by what they brought back with them: blistered sunburns that invoked jealousy, frizzing blond cornrows that showed off red strips of angry scalp underneath, puka-shell necklaces they wore tight around their necks as chokers. These were badges of pain and privilege. "Ohmygod, I'm peeling so bad," these girls and boys would proudly complain, gingerly picking at their reptile shoulders. "But my burns always turn into tans, so . . ."

What felt jarring wasn't the money spent, because money, to me, became incomprehensible in sums of more than twenty dollars. I had been steadily babysitting and working part-time at a Pei Wei Asian Diner, and considered myself rich because I could buy the large size of a frozen drink during study sessions at a chain coffee shop every week, and, every few months, I could go to T.J. Maxx and buy a pair of low-rise Paper Denim & Cloth jeans or a going-out top from the sale rack at Charlotte Russe. In a theoretical sense, I knew that money in large, mysterious quantities was a major part of adult life, and that the business of acquiring and saving it must be shameful or dull—likely both—because no one talked about it. It had to be why Chinese people like my parents always seemed to have money for things like homes and college educations but not for new shoes or books you didn't have to return to the library. To me, what being rich was really about—what really signaled wealth—was how easily one could spend money casually and with ease, on going out to eat at restaurants on days that weren't special occasions, or adding a pack of gum to the conveyor belt at checkout, or buying clothes with tags that weren't covered in layers of stickers, a stratigraphy of time spent being discounted. (As a kid, I had assumed that adults did not buy new clothes—that new clothes were purchased only once old clothes stopped fitting, and since my parents never fluctuated in size, that's why they still wore the same things they first brought to America.)

Sometime after we came back from that trip to China, something changed. I had always known Qing to be a typical immigrant mom when it came to fashion, spendthrift and conservative, dressing in the same few outfits I had assumed she had worn since the beginning of time. But, after we came home, Qing began shopping for herself. It started with her shopping for me. Beginning my freshman year of high school, we went on "sprees"—Qing and I would spend hours at the semiannual sale at Express, combing through each item in the 70 percent–off cardboard bins and leaving with giant bags I'd struggle to carry to the car, literally overflowing with abundance. She would encourage me to take risks: a black mesh turtleneck, an ultra-mini miniskirt, a low-cut top that I naively believed I'd one day fill out. Here and there, she would pick up an item for herself—a crocheted shrug with paillette sequins, a Pepto-pink shell embellished with hard-to-launder gold beads, new shoes that made her look younger than her age, for once.

The ease with which she fell into this shocked me. Up until then, I had known her as someone who only cared about clothes insofar as they were clean. I had not understood that the past decade and a half had been a break from habit, that this was a return to form. Soon, she began wearing jewelry again, and bought an engagement ring with a real diamond. She started painting her toenails a glossy cherry red. We even began eating at Applebee's for no reason at all, other than the fact that none of us had homework to do, and no one felt like cooking. There, Qing would always order dessert—chocolate lava cake, New York–style cheesecake, brownies and crème brûlées—and ask the waitress that hers arrive with everyone else's entrées.

But if these incidental frivolities were small drops in a bucket, then the time-share was a deluge. What disconcerted me was that I sincerely could not determine whether these vacations were frivolous or not. On one hand, it was an investment—the brochures said so—which connoted something prudent and responsible, and gave me faith that things had not gone sideways, that this was not one of those midlife crises I had read about that happened to someone else's parents. But on the other hand, how could this time-share be anything but pure nothingness? The idea of paying any amount of money to do something noneducational, where I might even get to wear a bikini, was, by itself, exhilarating—but knowing that my parents had made that choice undercut the thrill. What did Qing and Dexin know about time-shares that I didn't? Or, the more terrifying question, the one that I didn't want to think about: What *didn't* they know that I did?

"Beach vacations for the rest of our lives," Dexin crowed. I didn't even know if Qing owned a bathing suit.

I had not gone on spring break, even though most of my best friend group in high school went to Florida our senior year. It was a big deal for us, a mix of straight boys and girls, who had the sort of pragmatic approach to all aspects of life—grades, dating, prom, college, partying—of the old-fashioned good sense of people depicted in PSAs we'd watch in health class. We paired up for school dances based on a collective understanding of who made the most sense with whom (there was a list one of us kept), we made flash cards and shared them to study, we did not do drugs, those who drank did so only in basements, and the boys went to the local tanning salon to get base-layer tans before they left for spring break, so their burns wouldn't be as painful. I did everything else except for spring break, and I cannot remember the reason I gave my friends, but there was only one real reason: I did not go on vacation to have fun. Not allowed, not permitted, not possible. I don't even think I asked my parents—the answer was too obvious; the question would be evidence that I had lost my mind.*

The closest thing I had experienced to a vacation until that point was a summer I spent between my junior and senior years of high school at a chamber music retreat. In spite of my hatred for piano, I was adept at it, having studied with a Russian piano teacher who would often remind me that my master-pupil lineage traced all the way back to Beethoven, a factoid that was supposed to be inspiring but filled me with guilt. I could sight-read most music as long as it wasn't beyond my fingers' technical abilities, and I was considered very good by normal standards. This skill earned me the most unpopular kind of prestige: I was regularly asked to accompany the school choir for performances, participate during talent shows to balance out all the "lip sync dances," and be a part of the high school jazz band, even though I could not play any music that had not been written down exactly as it should be played, which made improvisation impossible—a handicap that turned my whole jazz experience into a grim and terrorizing one. But one spring,

---

*While fact-checking this book, it turns out that I had misremembered: Rori, Samira, and Juls did not go to this senior-year spring break either for various reasons—Rori's mom was undergoing chemo; Samira's mom thought it was frivolous—and it was humbling, yet again, to realize that I'm usually wrong about how special I am.

my piano teacher told me he was organizing a student trip to the Amalfi Coast along with the classical music department at the University of Illinois. We'd first train for two weeks in Champaign, two hours south of Chicago. Afterward, we'd fly to Italy and play concerts in Ravello, Capri, and Pompeii; Positano would be our home base.

I had no idea what the Amalfi Coast was, much less Positano. I was just thrilled that the years in which I had honed this despicable craft were finally going to pay off with an adventure, and that I'd get to travel somewhere warm, by the water, and unencumbered by my family. But when we arrived at the cliffside hotel, I thought that something had gone terribly wrong—that we must be in the wrong place because this place was *not nice*. The streets were narrow and paved in cobblestones, the buildings dilapidated and too close together. Our rooms were like caves—the walls were literally made of stone and felt damp—and the bathrooms seemed even older than the one in my laolao's apartment. But after we played our first gig at an unassuming restaurant and sat down to eat something, I realized that I was deeply mistaken: I couldn't find any entrée on the menu I could afford, so I ordered the cheapest thing, which was twenty euros. When it arrived, a fried something the size of my big toe, I was so shocked I didn't even complain. Afterward, I went to the corner store and bought enough bread and sandwich meat to last me the rest of the two weeks, and marveled at how much I didn't understand about the appearance of things and their value.

✦

In 2007, two years after that fateful day at the mall, we began taking annual family trips to resorts around the continent. (Our first year in the time-share program was a flop. We went to what we thought was Daytona Beach, but the resort, which was more like a motel, ended up being miles outside of the city. There were only two restaurants within walking distance, and both required us to sprint across the freeway right outside its front entrance—but the beach itself was a postcard paradise, with white sand so fine it felt like table salt running through my fingers, and still blue water that was the exact temperature of the inside of my own body.) When these trips began in earnest, I was in my second year of college at University of California, Berkeley, my sixth or seventh choice, and one I wasn't particularly excited to attend. I hadn't even visited the campus before I accepted, because I was so confident that I would make it into at least *one* of the "top" schools I had dreamed about. But when I clicked on the email from Berkeley and realized it was an acceptance letter, I cried. Not because I was relieved, though I was, but because it felt humiliating to be relieved after so

many rejections. There, I was less a student than a scam artist, using the same strategies that helped me slip my way
through high school with top honors, relying on memory
tricks to accurately parrot information to score well on tests,
employing big words and impressive-sounding sentences to
cover up my lack of original thought, even figuring out how
to snooze in lectures with my eyes open (thick contact lenses
can keep your eyes moist for an hour, even if you never
blink).

I liked California mostly because it was not Minnesota.
But I was not sure I understood Californians my own age,
who began conversations by asking each other what made
them happy and gave answers that sounded like they were
making fun of my answer (mine: blogging and reading
blogs, thinking about moving to New York to work in fashion after I graduated, putting together cool outfits; theirs:
being outside, spending quality time with good friends,
working with their hands). I thought everyone sounded
vaguely southern, and everyone thought I sounded vaguely
German. I felt very much out at sea, confused about these
supposedly ambitious people who didn't already know what
kind of careers they wanted for themselves and seemed
turned off by discussing the qualities that had gotten them
accepted to Berkeley in the first place. I did not realize how
much of a culture shock it was until a friend of mine who
also loved fashion asked me if I was going to study abroad,

and I answered with the truth, which I had not really considered before then: that going to school in California was enough of a study-abroad experience. Besides, I could not waste my parents' money, which paid for everything so I could get this degree, so I could get a job, so I could be successful and financially independent—and I would accomplish all this by not going to class and instead tending to my blog!

I crammed two majors' worth of credits into three years and spent my summers interning in the hopes that my job-hunting experience would be better than my college-hunting one. I focused all my energy on graduating early with a reasonable GPA, filling up my résumé with impressive-sounding stints, and getting out of the Bay Area. I had left Minnesota to find my people, and it made me angry that I hadn't. I isolated myself because I was on a different track—a better track, certainly, though I'd never admit it to these sunshine-loving freaks—and I couldn't wait until I could graduate, fly to New York City, start working on something that mattered, and finally start living.

I showed up to that first resort vacation after a particularly harried finals season, during which I went through my scammer's routine, which I had honed over three semesters, which was to get two potato pizzas at the Cheese Board when it opened at 8:00 a.m. and make a pot of strong coffee, which fueled me for the rest of my day when I'd attempt to learn five course loads of information within a week and rush through my papers, hoping I could finish everything before final exams and due dates. That December, I overdid it, and after a few days of this diet and pace, I headed to the bathroom in the early afternoon with a knot in my stomach and spent the next four hours curled up on the floor. A roommate drove me to the emergency room, where I tried to read in between bouts of pain until it was well past dark and the cramps had long subsided, and I finally saw a doctor who told me I was just dehydrated. I paid for the hospital bill with money I had made from blogging for a college gossip website so my parents wouldn't see it come through on their insurance statements.

I landed in Cancún feeling empty and ordinary. I had scored well enough on my tests and papers that it no longer burdened me, which meant I could forget everything I had learned and spend the rest of the holidays decompressing, relaxing, not caring. I was the exact kind of person these resorts hope enters their gates.

This resort was just like the ones we would visit in subsequent years, always in neon-bright beach towns of the kind of spring-break-type fantasy I watched on MTV with amazement: Miami Beach, Punta Cana, Honolulu. Although wherever we'd go, there we were: other Midwesterners, their shoulders mottled like overripe bananas under their Vikings, Packers, and Bears caps, along with immigrant families that looked exactly like us, four-person Chinese, Indian, Mexican, and Nigerian nuclear families, some with a grandparent in tow—new Americans newly inhabiting the upper middle class.

The resorts were all the same, though some were nicer than others. Our favorite locations were the ones on the coast of Mexico, giant sprawling places with tightly orchestrated evening entertainment, outdoor beds dressed in fresh white linens, and dramatic meandering boardwalks completely ensconced in planted palms and greenery that connected every building accessible to patrons and none that weren't. These resorts all had a surreal, placeless sameness to them. Whether it was in Mexico, Hawaii, the Caribbean, or elsewhere, the resort overwhelmed whatever local culture found its way in ("Gwa-see-us," Qing would always respond in thanks, even in Honolulu). Once, on my way home from Cancún, I realized I hadn't ever made it to the beach; in fact, I wasn't even sure if the resort was on the beach at all, or if we were even in Cancún, or an adjacent town nearby.

The opposite of Positano, these resorts were the most impressive upon first impression, the value obvious and unavoidable. The airport shuttle dropped us off in yawning canopied waiting areas with ceiling fans affixed to thatched roofs four stories above our heads that'd blow air we could not feel but nevertheless appreciated as we were simultaneously cooled by some hidden AC unit. From there, we'd take smaller shuttles to the hotel lobby, which would always be on the other side of the resort, and we'd have to take a private road to get there, drinking in the feeling of dense wind billowing out our airplane clothes, the sight of green and growing things quickly rushing by. During the check-in process, which was always quick and efficient, we'd receive our member wristbands, itineraries for day-long excursions, and an invitation to a free luxury breakfast so we could learn more about the time-share program. The rooms themselves were outfitted for the self-sufficient family, with dulled cooking pans and miniature bottles of dish soap, extra fleece blankets in the linen closets, and lawn furniture on the decks that was clean but rusted. Qing found that the housekeepers not only understood the rationale behind her typically bizarre requests, but were excellent coconspirators, too—in exchange for keeping the DO NOT DISTURB sign up for the entirety of our trip (Qing's obsessive early-morning cleanliness made any extra help unnecessary), we got a bounty of clean towels, trash bags, soap, and paper towels up front that'd last us the entire stay.

As a family, we approached these trips with a completist mindset, pressuring ourselves to enjoy every conceivably enjoyable thing without spending additional money. Qing, though, took this to new limits. Like a contestant on *Supermarket Sweep*, she was busier at these resorts than she was in her nonvacation life, in a quest to maximize her return on investment—every appetizer was consumed, every second of sunlight was soaked, every Astroturfed corner was photographed. When Julia and I would wake up in the afternoon, she'd regale us with stories from the past seven hours. No detail was too tedious: what the sunrise had looked like, what the seagulls had done that morning and then that afternoon, which of the other early risers she had befriended and what their daily dramas entailed. In Aruba, she met one woman, a chatty lady from Michigan whose skin was not so much sunburned as sundried, who confessed to Qing that she had already been at the resort for a month. "She was sad to go home," Qing told my sister and me over breakfast. We were horrified. We had been there only three days and had already run out of things to do.

The way I saw it, the main problem with these resorts was also its most effective pleasure principle, which is that there is nothing to distract you from the pervasive ubiquity of niceness. There is no opportunity to feel discomfort, disgust, or even inconvenience (and if you did feel that way, that was your problem, not the resort's). This quality was fastidiously maintained, the human effort largely invisible if you weren't looking for it, and most people were not. Once, I woke up from a nap in the early evening on the beach under a palapa as most patrons had already packed up and headed inside, and watched a hotel employee using a broom to sweep dried grass that had blown onto the beach into tidy piles to be bagged and disposed of.

Lulled by these amenities, we tourists are swaddled by these resorts. Leisure becomes both the pursuit and the product, packaged and presented as so much is in this country: to relieve you of pain, at a price. They keep those who stay there calm, blank, and empty. It is, even now, how most people travel—paying for the opportunity to do nothing, feel nothing, and disconnect. Travel is, for many, about aggressively going after your right not to have to be aggressive. This is as appealing for families new to the concept of forced leisure (like mine was) as it is for people who feel both overwhelmed and uninspired. For immigrant families in particular, there is an obvious appeal to this kind of numb erasure. It offers enough amenities that feel like the type of reward we had been suffering toward. *We made it. We paid money to do nothing.*

But as much as I longed to enjoy these resorts that my parents had worked so hard to bring us to, I found it impossible. One thing, in particular, always forced me to confront the truth of what unsettled me about these vacations: the inevitable "free breakfasts." They were not technically mandatory, but there would certainly be self-injurious consequences, we were told, if we didn't go—and so we gamely signed up for these breakfasts during which a time-share associate would attempt to upsell us "points" by taking us out to the resort's nicest buffet. We were plied with freebies from the churro bar, or the omelet bar, or the parfait bar as we listened to men smelling of spray deodorants try to make small talk with Dexin. My dad would get swept up by the energy of the banter, thrilled to venture a question that would then be met with an enthusiastic attempt at what seemed like a thorough answer. It frustrated me to see him fall prey to such transparently machismo salesmanship. But then it'd strike me that being the recipient of such reverent attention must not happen often to Dexin, and I'd feel suddenly chastened.

At these fake-casual outings, I began to notice how resort salespeople ignored Qing with icy precision, setting their forearms on the table when they looked at Dexin as their pitches grew serious, except for the one moment they would inevitably turn to Qing with a perfectly timed smile to tell her that she could be my sister. Qing's smile was so tight her eyes would be forced closed, and she'd bury her head into her second omelet. These meals were an onslaught of Things That Were Embarrassing. That we wouldn't be eating here if it weren't free. That we should absolutely not buy more points, but we might. Dexin's eagerness. Qing's gluttony. That I couldn't participate in the conversation, even if I wanted to. That despite the resorts being real and as advertised, this whole thing was a scam.

Here is the gist: Time-shares offer multiple families the

enjoyment of a single vacation home, arranged so each family owns a fraction of the home in weeks and months, not square footage. The basic principle is exploded to account for many millions of families and thousands of properties, but these time-share programs simplify all this with the introduction of points: By translating your stake in the time-share to points that are replenished each year, you can spend them like cash on booking accommodations on the time-share's proprietary reservation system.

The logic goes that this system gets you convenient access to vacations that normally would cost much more. Within a sprawling time-share program, you get treated like a VIP, because you're not just a tourist—you're an *owner.* And, like homeownership, the money time-sharers spend on vacations is an investment, because, technically, you can sell or sublet your equity—your points—to other people.

But what other people? When asked about unloading points during years we wanted to take vacations outside of the program, Dexin was told that it wasn't wise: "There's not really a market to resell *these* points, but there is if you convert them into these *other* points, which we don't recommend because of the surcharge, but we can explore that option if you're interested." There were annual maintenance fees to pay, even if you didn't use your points, and Dexin could never figure out how to trade or sell off unused points on the indecipherable internal portal that seemed to have been first built in the nineties and never updated. Business, it seemed, relied on selling more points to those who already owned some, rather than recruiting new owners. Eventually, the kiosk in the mall disappeared, and I wondered which new-immigrant city the corporation had moved on to.

Many years later, I was working with a freelance videographer who told me that he regrets only two projects he's ever taken on for a paycheck: one, for some side business operated by Donald Trump in the mid-2000s, and another, a commercial for a Mexican resort. The resort job didn't pay especially well, but he didn't mind initially since it was a free trip. Yet the more he worked with the team, the more he felt like his job was to sell the resort to customers who could not afford it. "Honestly, I felt dirtier afterward than I did after I shot the Trump one." He pulled up photos on his phone. It was the same place my family had gone to in Cancún.

During one free breakfast, I listened as conversation circled the subject of upgrading our points package—that by paying just a few hundred more a year, we could be vacationing twice a year in Tahiti, Côte d'Azur, or the Amalfi Coast. These were not places that rang any bells for my parents, but Dexin still grinned. Qing smiled her tight-lipped grimace again at the wrong times, smartly feigning deafness and dumbness.

"My dad's just being polite," I finally said, as seriously as I could muster. "We're here for the free breakfast."

The salesperson laughed, pushing himself forward to balance on two chair legs, his tone taking on a syrupy affectation. "You sure tell it like it is! But you'll inherit these points one day, so you should pay attention, too."

"I *have* been paying attention!" I said more forcefully, surprising everyone but mostly myself. "Nothing you've said makes *any* sense." I had the pretend-confidence of a child before a tantrum. "I'm serious," I insisted, with tears now in my eyes.

The next year, after the second time I ended a sales meal in hysterics, my parents told me we'd stop going to these breakfasts. We dodged the phone calls that would arrive every morning and started making a game of hiding from the various salespeople who were assigned to our account. It had now become funny, though it still made me queasy, how easily we had become chumps, and I chose not to think about it if I could help it.

I'VE LONG JOKED that I am unscammable. That as soon as I get a whiff that someone wants me to join, to sign up, to invest, to commit, I am out of there. One of my earliest vivid memories was of being invited to a trampoline playgroup that my friend Miyo would talk about on our bus ride to and from the elementary school. When her mom dropped the two of us off on a Wednesday evening, I realized that the trampolines were just bait and that I was actually at a Bible study, and the counselors required us to memorize a psalm—whatever that was—before we were allowed to play. "It's *so* easy," Miyo encouraged me, telling me she had memorized dozens already. I looked down at the sheet in front of me, at these poems that were half in English. Some sentences seemed to be written backward, full of incomprehensible words that resembled words I knew, but were not, which made me feel like I had gone insane. Normally a quick study, not to mention a greedy reader, I struggled even to sound the words aloud, watching as every other kid quickly recited a psalm to an adult and then sprinted to the trampolines. I don't remember whether I eventually did memorize anything, or if I eventually got to use those trampolines, but I remember that I never spoke to Miyo again.

It's a sensitivity that my sister and I both have—a nose for being made a fool, a sixth sense for being taken advantage of. Most of the time, I have no idea what the scam is, but I know well enough when someone is desperate for me to take an action I normally wouldn't, and that's enough: It's how a question is delivered, or that something is just a little too convenient, or when an off-the-cuff anecdote sounds just slightly rehearsed or follows a too-long delay—the right pattern of three dots that pop up and disappear when they're texting and stop. My husband, far more trusting and less foreign than I am, who did not grow up feeling the need to be his parents' cultural translator and watchdog, has gotten us entangled in a handful of minor scams with amateur locksmiths, auto body work done in parking lots, and Craigslist wire transfers. I have likely self-sabotaged many real opportunities because my scam detector has been calibrated to be too sensitive, but I cannot help it.

I never said anything to Qing, of course. I knew how stuck we were, and I believed that talking about it would only make us feel worse about our foolishness. During the same vacation in which I threw my breakfast tantrum, I grew more and more glum until one day, while we were sitting next to the pool (Dexin and Julia had gone back to the room to nap), Qing could no longer take it. "You think you are better?" she said, looking around the pool at copies of our family—a rainbow of brown, tan, and pink backs and bellies.

I was thankful that I had dark sunglasses on. She continued: "If you do not want to be here, go. You talk like you cannot leave here. That this place is bad to everyone, all guests. But you are the only person with pain right now. You act like you are different. And yes, you are special. It's *really*. But you are not better."

I looked down at my hands. The tops of them had burned, which was not a surprise since I had refused to apply any sunscreen so I could achieve as deep a tan as possible. In the light of the resort bathrooms, I looked bronzed and healthy, as close to the photos of women modeling summer swim trends as I could get. But underneath the harsh sunshine, my skin was barely recognizable, splotchy and dead-looking, and the large spots that had burned appeared mottled against the bones in my hands.

"You know Miyo?" Qing finally said.

"I guess . . ." I started. "She tricked me."

"She was your friend. You had only one friend in elementary school, Kate, and then you had no friends. Miyo was a new friend, and then she was not. You think about why?"

"That's really mean, Mom."

"Not mean. Listen to me. You decide you cannot be friends with her. You decide same thing with many other kids wanting to be friends. Because you think you are better."

We gazed out across the artificial beach, but I could not see. I was angry, and I was angry with Qing, but that was not it. I couldn't understand who I was angry with, or where it was coming from, just that I was. I *had* been made a fool, but maybe I did it to myself. And here was Qing suggesting that the most foolish thing is to act like I wasn't foolish. Was I too principled to enjoy a lazy afternoon in the sunshine? To appreciate the family time, which was what the brochures advertised? To actually learn how the world worked instead of pretending I already knew? Acid tears slid out beneath my sunglasses and singed my already tender nose, lips, and chin.

"You are not a kid anymore. But you still believe this story."

# FOUR

# Amusement Bounders
## *Disney World*

When I turned nine, Qing started a full-time job working as an accountant for a logistics and transportation corporation, and she implemented a new rule at home regarding TV. Julia and I were allowed to watch only thirty minutes a day, a rule I was partially excited to obey, because I'd get to complain about it along with the other kids at school. We chose to performatively utilize those thirty minutes in front of our parents ("I think I'll use it on *20/20* tonight"), but when Qing and Dexin were at work, all bets were off. Especially during the summer, Julia and I spent nearly every minute our parents weren't at home in front of the TV set—me on the carpet with the big toe of my right foot on the channel changer and Julia splayed out on the couch. We'd watch cartoons in the morning, soaps in the early afternoon, and then *Ricki Lake*, *Sally*, and *Maury* as we ate our lunch. There was dead time between those programs and when my parents came home, in which nothing but infomercials were on, and when we grew tired of those, that's when we'd re-watch our favorite VHS tapes: Disney's Sing-Along Songs. These tapes were ancient, far older than me when I was watching them, and interspersed between songs from *The Jungle Book*, *Snow White*, and *Peter Pan*, there were other more bizarre songs, from movies the kids from school didn't know, like "Zip-a-Dee-Doo-Dah" from *Song of the South*, about a Black man at a Reconstruction-era plantation at which he had been recently enslaved and cheerfully mentors a young white kid through the various boyhood challenges he faces—or "The Siamese Cat Song" from *Lady and the Tramp*, in which twin cats with buck teeth and slanted eyes plot to murder a goldfish: "Maybe we could reaching in and make it drown," they'd hiss in broken English.

We loved these tapes. We watched them before either of us had ever seen a full-length Disney film, and even after we saw one—we got the VHS of *Beauty and the Beast* and had to turn it off before the halfway point because the two of us had burst into hysterics during the forest scene in which Belle's father's caravan is overturned—we still preferred the

Sing-Alongs. These tapes were like candy: satisfying and stirring, but so processed and decontextualized that they were as representative of real Disney movies as Gushers are of real fruit. The point of songs, in any musical, is to highlight emotional peaks and valleys. But Sing-Alongs removed the songs from the plot, turning each one into a frozen moment that gestured at the existence of big feelings—without demanding that the listener even feel a small feeling. We also enjoyed the Sing-Along subtext, to the extent that we could have possibly understood it with our adolescent brains and hearts: that during times of crises, loneliness, and change, it would not be a knight in shining armor that would save us. All you need to be a hero is the skill and imagination to escape inward, the ability to re-narrate events for yourself in real time, to visualize animated birds around you when there's nothing but dust.

And besides, if a song contained enough of the plot that the princess's sadness or Mickey's panic broke our numb reverie, it was easy enough to move my big toe over to the fast-forward button.

You would think, then, that a trip to Disney World would have been some kind of dream come true—an extravagance with semifamiliar elements in an environment constructed purely for amusement, not education. The fact is, I do not remember much about being there for the first time, when we made the drive from Tuscaloosa to Orlando.

At that point, I had developed a tendency toward shyness, and my parents were deeply concerned. So Qing devised a sort of educational program that required me to talk to adults at every opportunity I got. During get-togethers among all the Chinese families in town, I had to—before leaving—approach the host āyí to convey how appreciative I was to be invited to her home, and that the food was delicious. At restaurants, I'd be forced to order for the whole family. On road trips, I'd have to find a tour guide or a docent—a security guard if no one else was around—to ask a question I was never really curious about. Once, on a trip to New England, we found ourselves on a series of college tours alongside other families with teenage children there to visit prospective schools. "When was Harvard built?" eight-year-old me asked, my voice warbling like there was a gun aimed at my head.

The photos of me from this first trip to Disney World capture this torturous exercise. I had asked Belle a question but spoke too quietly for her to hear, so she leaned over to listen, her flummoxed face frozen in Canon film (likely, I asked her something like "What do you like most about Disney World?" or "What college did you go to?"). Subsequent photos depict my reaction to the awkward exchange, a dissociative stare while I pressed play on my internal Sing-Along machine.

It was not all a wash: At Julia's insistence (she was two),

we spent most of the time riding It's a Small World in circles—listening to the song from her favorite Sing-Along tape as many times in a row as she wanted, piped in fresh from the source, through two dozen tinny speakers spread along an indoor river, with puppets attached to spinning cogs clicking their wooden clogs under windmills, dancing the cancan on a stage, flying through the air on magic carpets, and then—the music suddenly underpinned with gongs—doing acrobatics on top of panda bears and bowing in kimonos. Qing remembers that, at some point, the ride operators just let us remain in our floating car instead of getting out to queue again. For months afterward, no one was allowed to play Sing-Alongs around Dexin.

"It feels like Disneyland" is how people describe places that feel artificial. By the time I was ready to decide where I would live as an adult, I chose to go to the least Disney place I could think of. And so, the day after I walked across the stage to graduate from Berkeley, I moved to New York City.

I had been to New York before, most recently on a field trip with the high school jazz band, where we performed to an empty auditorium inside an aircraft-carrier-turned-war-museum, and also to an empty auditorium inside Carnegie

Hall. But then we went to the Blue Note as an audience for a matinee performance, and I had never experienced anything like it: to be among so many people who had chosen, on a beautiful sunny day, to sit in a windowless club. Who had chosen to gather here in order to quietly witness talented and passionate people try the very hardest they could.

In retrospect, it strikes me that this was the first moment in which I felt like I had found a place where I could belong. I did not like jazz, I was not with friends, no one was looking at me or paying special attention to me. And yet I felt a deep kinship to this place, like I was made out of the same cherry-wood lacquer as the chair I sat on. That evening, I linked up with a trumpet player and a saxophone player; we left our hotel in Times Square and scooped through Hell's Kitchen, and then shot up on Sixth Avenue, walking past the Empire State Building and Bryant Park, which I recognized from the fashion blogs I read. We hardly talked as we walked, which freaked us all out, as we did not really know how to be teenagers who could survive without relentless low-stakes chatter. The trumpet player said he was going to head back, which suited me just fine, as I had a not-small crush on the saxophone player, who told me, once we were alone, that he *thought* he really liked New York, but he was having a hard time figuring out why, which didn't happen to him much. I felt the same way.

After I graduated from college, I arrived in New York City with two suitcases and a bad case of food poisoning, having eaten something questionable during my journey. At the luggage carousel, a man dressed in a faded suit with oily patches approached me and said that he wasn't supposed to do this—his boss wouldn't like it if he found out!—but his client had called to say he didn't need a ride from the airport anymore, and asked whether I needed a ride for a subsidized, very affordable rate of a hundred dollars ("It's New York! Cabs will charge you double, *at least*."). I followed him to his car, where I lay across the back seat, panting to prevent myself from throwing up, trying not to smell the now-dried remnants from a previous passenger who had been less successful. I arrived at my destination, an apartment of a friend of a friend who shared the space in Spanish Harlem with two Australian men, and she told me that there was a standard flat rate for cab rides out of JFK airport—she was pretty sure it was less than fifty dollars. "You're funny," she said, grinning, and handed me a beer. It turned out that my scam detector was faulty; it needed an NYC recalibration. "He won, you lost. It'll be your turn later," she told me, warmed by her own twenty-three-year-old wisdom.

She was right, and I won often and lost just as frequently, though I never fell for a black-car hustle again. But even losing in New York felt like a gift, in some way, because being able to say "you won't believe what happened to me" was currency. I began to enjoy trading misery with friends, and this kind of bonding through misfortune made so much more sense to me than the bonding through earnestness I had encountered in college. It *was* funny to go see a new dentist, who was a friend's father and who had promised to give me a good deal because he knew I didn't have health insurance, but then the bill came anyway, and it was $200, and when I called the office to tell them about the error, they informed me that *was* the discounted rate and the only thing I knew how to do was to burst into tears. It *was* hilarious that I called in to work to take a day off because my roommate had just learned that her ex-boyfriend was now with her best friend, an *unimaginable* betrayal, I relayed to my boss, who patiently listened to me describe what had happened, and then, very coolly, told me that I was free to take the day off, but I should know that it was a really stupid reason. It *was* funny to cry on the street and not have a single person interact with you, except to say with their eyes that they had been there, too. It was in New York that I began to associate invisibility with liberation. That the freest I could feel, the most me I could be, was when no one else cared to see me because there was so much more to look at.

In a way, I was pantomiming living: I had my own room, but no door; I had a pot that I used to boil eggs and make Annie's boxed macaroni and cheese, but chose to eat most of my meals outside the house, because it was cheaper to do that in the East Village than to grocery shop. Living in New York was hard, and the effort was physical—a stroll down my favorite street on the most beautiful, brilliant day still meant I had to hold my breath at certain intersections. It was not Disneyland to me, and would not feel like Disneyland for a very long time.

Part of the reason for that was how allergic New Yorkers seemed to be to phony things: People were poseurs, clout chasers, and cringe for pretending to be anything they were not naturally. Even using corporate jargon—to "touch base" with someone, to "circle back"—was embarrassing because being an authority pleaser meant you had no authority of your own. It was here that I first came across people who expected you to try hard, but only on unpleasant tasks: Try too hard to seek pleasure, comfort, or magic, and they'll start swapping bets on how long you'll last.

I was grateful to have learned how to embody this perspective, especially since my job as a fashion writer for *Refinery29* required phoniness. I had to walk a fine line between telling people how to dress like someone else and convincing them that they were dressing like themselves. Part of this work meant reporting on subcultures and their dress codes, which I'd approach as an armchair anthropologist (and also as a snob). Never did this come to more of a head than when I covered Disneybounders: the self-described term for adult Disney fans bound for the parks. The community formed around those who had discovered a creative loophole, a way to get around an official Disney policy that prohibited anyone over the age of fourteen from showing up to Disney theme parks in a costume lest young children confuse park guests for official Disney cast members who are trained to work with kids. Instead of wearing full costumes, these Disneybounders would put together "inspired by" versions of their favorite characters using their own closet staples and diligently document them for one another. It was no coincidence that there were few Disneybounders in New York; they knew they were not welcome.

I wrote and assigned articles about Disneybounders—what they wore to the parks, what Disneybounding helped them express about their own lives, the influencers who were making a name for themselves in Disney cosplay. As far as I could tell, these communities were incredibly supportive of one another, upbeat in everything they did, and enthusiastic about their pursuits, perhaps as a defense against the general repulsion directed at them by the anonymous internet. In the comments section of any article about Disneybounders were the same kind of criticism and insults: They were creepy because they obsessed over a children's product despite having no children themselves;

they were suckers for feeling such unadulterated fondness for one of the most powerful companies in the world; they were tacky for still wearing jersey circle skirts; they were Western supremacists who traveled all the way around the world only to remain within the gated walls of Shanghai Disney Resort; and, worst of all, they suffered from a pathological arrested development, a blind belief that happy endings happen to everyone, that performed joyfulness leads to actual joyfulness. Only someone truly out of touch could see people being paid minimum wage to wear foam heads and mechanically dance to choreographed numbers underneath a castle made out of molded plastic and call it magical.

I suspect that Disneybounders suffer from a similar prejudice that also applies to clowns. There are those who see a clown—someone resembling an adult who should technically behave and think like an adult, but who instead possesses a random assortment of capabilities, quirks, and responses acceptable only in two-year-olds—and laugh. Others are repelled (I consider myself mildly clownphobic). Disneybounders also contain a clown's mix of contradicting extremes—a person with the cleverness and dexterity to tie a balloon animal but the emotional immaturity to sob when the animal pops; a person with the self-realization and competency to recognize that they needed to create a more fulfilling life for themselves, only to move to a new town within walking distance to a theme park made for children so they could finally take their daily morning coffee with a Mickey macaron at the Jolly Holiday Bakery Cafe off Main Street, USA—that is fascinating, but also abjectly unsettling.

In person and off-screen, Disneybounders and other adult Disney enthusiasts I met were kind, genuine people, some with a wicked sense of self-aware irony—no less creepy or obsessive or stunted than the average person. A video shoot I worked on for *Refinery29*'s *Style Out There* brought me to Celebration, Florida, a planned city minutes away from Disney World that was originally intended to be the real-world manifestation of Walt Disney's core dogma, in which he thought the world should be less like American cities (dirty, disorganized, and crime-ridden), and more like his theme parks (pristine, orderly, and predictable), in which the ugly drudgeries of daily operations, everything from garbage disposal to mail delivery, should be hidden and discreet, and—ideally—not done by humans. There, I met hard-core Bounders who had created lives for themselves that centered around this hobby. Some had anxiety or mood disorders that they managed with Disney, a source of comfort they had relied on since childhood. Others just enjoyed studying and consuming Disney trivia and ephemera as one might approach Winston Churchill documentaries or the NCAA. Others, still, just liked the pageantry of dressing up in a costume that came ready-made with an activity, like the camaraderie that comes with piling into a car to go snowboarding with friends or getting ready together during a girls' trip in Vegas. They were not deluded that Disney World was the Actual World. They knew that Snow White also had a TikTok account in which she did sponcon for teeth-whitening services. Some of them confessed that they wouldn't have ever felt brave enough to leave the country if it hadn't been for Shanghai Disney Resort. To them, Disney did not protect them from the real world; it held their hands as they ventured into it.

Even so, Celebration was fake-feeling, even by Eden Prairie standards. Everything from the post office to the fire station looked like it came from a toy kit, and the restaurants that populated the city center broadly covered the major cuisine groups without overlap or competition. The man-made lake adjacent to the downtown was surrounded by a wide promenade lined with rocking chairs, and the producer told me that on December nights, artificial snow made from soap foam sprays out of hidden jets alongside the path and drifts all through town, carried by central Florida's sixty-degree winter breeze.

That trip was the first stop on a whirlwind excursion during which I would spend two months on and off the road filming *Style Out There*, a documentary series about fashion and beauty subcultures that expanded upon some of the ideas I had been exploring in my written work—why people dress to stand out; who considers themselves outsiders (and whether it's a self-imposed marginalization or one that's been forced upon them); how clothes can communicate what you can't bring yourself to say; and how personal identity and cultural exchange are messy affairs, and thus are incredible opportunities to empathize with and learn from those who live out their own truths and traditions instead of writing it all off as simply "problematic."

To this day, filming this show was the most difficult thing I have ever done in my career, and the most rewarding. It took many cities after Celebration before I became used to the shoots' frenetic travel schedules, falling asleep curled up in a plane seat somewhere over eastern Mexico and waking up in Windhoek, Namibia—and scrambling to finish a voiceover script describing the drag scene in Tel Aviv before we landed.

These trips were intense. We'd work fifteen-hour days and would try to sleep whenever we could. There was never time to sightsee. And so, from Kingston to Zacatecas, Hokes Bluff to Harajuku, I spent my time in intimate spaces I would have never gotten to see as a traveler—people's homes and studios, their weddings and get-togethers, the insides of their suitcases and closets and minds and hearts—and hardly any time at all in public spaces: the city squares built around stolen obelisks and monuments to conquests; the museums filled with the chosen artifacts that broadcast the exact right message of glory; the feats of infrastructure and engineering that were often replicas of what those in charge had been awestruck by while elsewhere, and so chose to clone it so they could own it. The traveling I did for *Style Out There* was as close as I'll ever come to seeing behind the traveler's curtain. Always drawn for company, this curtain presents a self-professed ideal—a planned authenticity that is, by nature, inauthentic.

I believe I did see and understand Celebration, the unfiltered, non-spit-shined place of its inhabitants' understanding, inhabitants who showed me their lives as they actually live them. And what was so disturbing to me was that despite the plastic veneer and the supermarket superficiality of its local culture, it was as true and distinct—which is to say that it's also as fake and referential—as most places on this planet.

"How is it?" Qing asked me on the phone during the last evening of our shoot in Florida. "It's nice?"

"It feels like Disney everywhere," I responded, gazing out my hotel room window into a nearly empty kidney-shaped swimming pool. There was a power line, just beyond the main road, in the shape of Mickey ears.

"Well, don't cry this time," she joked.

FIVE YEARS before this work trip, I had left Disney World for what I promised myself was my last time. We had spent one of our time-share holidays at a resort in Orlando to fête the arrival of Bin Bin, Qing's best friend's son who had gotten accepted into a master's program and would be in the United States for the foreseeable future. Bin Bin chose the English name Bowen for himself, a near approximation of his given Chinese name and one I had to look up when he told me, since I had never come across it in my life. He swore it was a real name, and he was right: Bowen is a Welsh name and has barely cracked the top one thousand most popular names given to American babies, but in recent decades, it's one of the top five English names given to baby boys in China. In Mandarin, Bowen is a homonym for a word that means "abundant, rich, and literate." Given the New England communities in which American-born Bowens are mostly found, the name seems to connote many of the same qualities here.

When Bowen first arrived in New York City to visit, I walked around Lower Manhattan with him near the *Refinery29* office. Like all new transplants, he couldn't stop looking up at the tall buildings, a habit that gets quickly beaten out of you the second or third time you get shoulder checked by another pedestrian who wants you to know they've been here longer. On the corner of Broadway and Ann Street, his gaze suddenly snapped downward. "I'm going to drive one of those one day," he stated, pointing at a limousine, all its windows heavily tinted.

"A limo? You mean you're going to *be* driven in one?"

"No, I'm going to drive it. I'm going to drive the biggest car, and that's a limousine." I started to correct him, but the smile on his face was so wide that I felt diffusely embarrassed, not at all about what he said, but rather how I felt about how he said it: logically, enthusiastically, and all wrong.

Our family would congregate in Orlando—Bowen and I flew in from New York, Julia from Los Angeles, and my parents from Minnesota—and planned to spend a full week at Disney World's various theme parks. It was our first trip as more than just our family unit of four, and the addition of another person threw us off balance. Bowen was naive, eager, callous, and creative. An only child in a country full of them, he was spectacularly spoiled yet under immense pressure to perform. He was drawn toward the accessible extravagances of American life, and unaware of what it took for my family to finally access it; he loved how liberated Americans were, how they spoke as freely about their own shortcomings and anxieties as they did their desires and hopes, but Bowen did not understand the nuances in decorum that distinguishes congenial people from those without boundaries. Walking around in just his boxers, ordering the most expensive thing off the menu, asking probing questions about old jobs and new relationships, Bowen was just enjoying the promise of an American Vacation, we kept telling each other.

But years of slowly adding one more requirement, pec-cadillo, consideration, and unacknowledged thing to the tabletop that was our family—balancing a fork on top of a mug, a bowl on top of a platter, a plate on top of all that—meant that we had no idea how delicate our dynamic was, how much weight we were each carrying, and how tenu-ously stacked our relationships were. I was working at a dream job that was also shrinking me, and finding solace in a new relationship that was beginning to profoundly change me. Julia was graduating from college soon, and feeling overwhelmed by the idea of spending another four years in medical school. Dexin was toiling away at a job that, it was becoming more and more apparent, came with a looming expiration date. At home, a still-recent empty nester, Qing could not ignore the concessions she had tried to make peace with, over and over, during the last two decades: She had offered her own independence, her obstinate whimsi-cality, her unclipped wings, so her children would have a winning chance at adulthood. And now that her job was technically done, she was beginning to realize that she did not know what was on the other side of that sacrifice. She was once again an autonomous person who existed for the sake of no one but herself. She was wearing clothes that drew attention and made her feel special, and she began to forgo cooking—a chore she despised—for eating individu-ally wrapped Dove chocolates by the bagful. But the person who looked back at her in the mirror was still not familiar to her. The reflection was a facsimile, a cosplay of who she had been. She felt every long, taxing year of the journey. But where had she arrived? Point B, she couldn't help but fear, was a dancing, flickering mirage of Point A—a fake moon reflected by the resort pool underneath the real one in the night sky. One fallen leaf, and she'd know how unsolid she had become.

Our Orlando trip started at Epcot, a theme park dedicated to the "celebration of human achievement," meant to honor the diverse innovations in planned communities. It is all very cerebral for a theme park, which is why the "theme" of Epcot is probably the least effable one of all. As you walk through the various pavilions dedicated to France (complete with a miniature Eiffel Tower), Mexico (featuring a scaled-down Mayan pyramid), and Canada (with a miniature version of the Château Frontenac), there are roller coasters and rides for *Kim Possible*, *Finding Nemo*, *Ratatouille*, and *Guardians of the Galaxy*. One gets the sense that the communities found in fictional outer space, or among the rats who lived under Gusteau's floorboards, or in animated Middleton, USA, are as exotic, impressive, and improbable as the ones in Morocco, Norway, or China. Even America gets the Epcot treatment: Located between Italy and Japan, the American Adventure includes a Muppet-themed barbecue restaurant and a "Heritage Manor" constructed in the colonial style and filled with statues that personify twelve American values, including compassion, immigration, Westward expansion, and wartime collectivism.

But the majority of our week was spent within Magic Kingdom park, walking up and down Main Street, circling Cinderella Castle, standing in hours-long lines to briefly sit inside teacups, haunted elevators, and riverboats. If Epcot's intellectual ambition is to tell a story about human achievement, then Magic Kingdom's story is about human imagination, and the fairy tales and dreams we rely on in order to fuel those achievements. Even in the most mundane, pedestrian ways, I saw how much the promise works: There are few reasons one would ever stand in line for hours to enjoy a five-minute experience. Experiencing magic is one such reason. Paying for tickets and feeling compelled to get your money's worth is an equally motivating one. I can't decide which one is more American.

It had been a long week at Disney World, and our last day was interminable. Our excursions had taken on a routine quality, which calcified everything in staleness. The odor of funnel cakes began to smell like sweet poison in my nose, and every last square inch of my body ached. I began to hear Disney songs even when I knew there were none playing, the ghostly aftertaste imprinted into my eardrums. After a week of eating only burgers, corn dogs, and pizza, I whined that we ought to leave the grounds to get dinner before the holiday fireworks show that evening, a demand that was easier said than done because the physical act of leaving the park—weaving our way through the crowds to the exit, taking the shuttle to the lot where we parked, idling in traffic to exit the gates—would take at least two hours. Coming back would take even longer. But I had had enough of the Happiest Place on Earth. Qing called me a brat, and so I became one, refusing to walk with the family, entertain any question, respond to any stimuli. Even Bowen, who had been unfazed by nearly everything else up until this point, stopped trying to lighten the mood. After an hour of me sulking, the family finally gave in, and we slid toward the exit and ate a forgettable meal somewhere close to the resort. We went back to the resort to change our clothes before the fireworks that night, each person feeling like they had lost the battle in a deeply annoying way.

I had been waiting at the door to my parents' room, dressed in a polka-dot dress that was the most festive thing I had brought, willing myself to drop it and have a good time. It was too much work to stay as mad as I was, and I genuinely liked fireworks. Plus, Qing wasn't the enemy, anyway. So, when she emerged from the room wearing a pair of polka-dot pants, I made a joke: "Hey, you're copying me!"

Without looking at me, she spun on her heels and went back to her room. I glanced at my dad, who went in after her. After too brief a time, he came back out. "Mom doesn't want to go anymore," he relayed with a shrug.

I barreled past him, newly incensed and righteous. I had been the adult here, having just decided to play nice. She was being a child in her typical fashion—leaping to illogical conclusions, insisting on malicious intent, and that pissed me off—and over something as dumb as, what, pants? The suggestion that our clothes matched? Of kinship? Her not going meant that none of us would go—that's just how we behaved, and I knew that she knew it—and I felt it was a spectacularly petty and spiteful thing she was doing to me, taking away the only enjoyable event of the day, after the kind of day we had had. I pushed open the door.

Qing was curled up on the made-up bed, in a shrimp shape. She was perfectly silent and still, but I realized that she was actually in furious motion, her whole body convulsing in tiny piston movements. She was sobbing. The words that I had ready turned into vapor.

"Mom?" I finally ventured.

After some moments, her shoulders stilled, but she did not unfurl.

I continued to stand in the doorway until the shrimp shape spoke. "You can say many things about Mom. That I am *weird*. That I do not know about things. But I never copy," she said with fire. "You have no idea what Mom's life is. What I do—did—so you can act like people *want* to copy *you*."

I stood there in silence. From the living room, Bowen coughed.

Qing sat up in bed and turned around to face me. Her face was swollen, pale with red blotches. "Mom does not want to be *you*."

"Why not?" I whispered.

"*Because*." A pause, the effort like running through glue. "Because I want—*I want* to be me."

It was not an insult, nor a cry for help. Qing was sharing. I sat on the bed next to her, and she let me.

I heard Bowen open the refrigerator for a drink and turn on the television.

"We're leaving now," Qing said, suddenly standing up. "Let's go," she said over her shoulder as she walked toward the front door. The rest of us scurried to find our jackets and shoes, copying her efficient movements. It took us an hour to reenter the park, and the show started nearly as soon as we made our way inside. On Main Street, twinkle-light-trimmed trolleys packed with cast members sang and danced under a sky full of fireworks, the biggest display I had ever seen. The contacts in my eyes were thick and schmaltzy from dried tears, and the contrast between the artificial lights and the darkness of night made everything dreamlike, surrounded by halos—the impression of fireworks on my corneas lasting much longer than the actual gunpowder in the sky. It was corny, and so lovely.

Walking back to the car, I vowed to never go back to Disney World—knowing full well that it was a promise I couldn't keep, and would eventually, perhaps and god willing, not want to. I might have kids. They might want to go. Disney might make them happy in ways it did not for me. Or maybe they'd feel the exact same way. Who knew what my life would be?

It was not happily ever after, but my body—gentle, content, on tiptoes and pliant knees and ready to catch myself no matter which direction I tipped—insisted that this was something even better: a blank page, a known unknown, and a certainty that the fiction we sing to ourselves during moments we know are being etched into our bones, changing the acidity of our blood, rewiring our heartstrings, couldn't be even half as meaningful as what actually is and will be.

# FIVE

# Thrill Seekers
## *Las Vegas*

One of Qing's favorite movies is *Magic Mike XXL*, the 2015 sequel to the Steven Soderbergh–directed 2012 *Magic Mike*. In the original, a young college dropout is introduced to the universe of male stripping by the eponymous Mike, an entrepreneurial but depressive dancer played by Channing Tatum, whose own life as an ambitious Tampa stripper loosely inspired the screenplay. After a series of drug-fueled disasters in the pursuit of financial independence, Mike finally extracts himself from the downward spiral in order to pursue a less volatile (and more clothed) profession as a furniture maker. It's a Cinderella tale in reverse, and surprisingly sensitive and introspective—an art film disguised as a beefcake flick, and exactly the opposite of its sequel *Magic Mike XXL*, which is a road-trip movie that is *also* a beefcake flick, filled with haphazard cameos of shirtless celebrities, dizzying choreography, and juvenile hijinks, and little of the barbed truth-telling of the original. If the first *Magic Mike* is a slow burn, the second is an M-80 stuffed into a pumpkin.

Qing first saw *Magic Mike XXL* in the Eden Prairie AMC theater with Dexin, who, to this day, offers his sole opinion of the movie by shaking his head whenever it's brought up, which is often. After this initial viewing, Qing began mentioning it during the daily phone calls I made to her as I walked from the subway stop back to my apartment in Brooklyn: *I like how Channing Tatum makes everyone around him feel positive and good. Any man who doesn't like this movie is just jealous! Do you think Channing Tatum is not afraid of old women in real life, either?*

Tired of the lack of enthusiasm from her own family members, Qing tried to organize a group viewing for some of the other Chinese women she was friendly with in Eden Prairie—a huge risk, considering the other activities that encompassed the totality of their social life: nature walks, tai chi practice, and potluck dinners. To Qing's chagrin, nearly everyone declined. Days later, she fumed to me on the phone: "Name one bad thing that happened in the movie! You cannot! There is not one bad thing. There is not even DRUGS."

I couldn't bring myself to tell Qing that drug use was one of the only overlapping themes between the two Magic Mike movies—specifically, what happens when you take Molly at the wrong time. But, then again, that was the basis of so much of our relationship: We pretend "bad things" don't exist, and even when confronted with them, we pretend that we're too naive to recognize them for what they were. We did this with lots of things—money problems, family secrets, hurt feelings, hurt bodies. Once, when I was ten, Qing broke her leg. While rushing out of the house to a final exam for her degree, she slipped and fell, snapping both tibia and fibula so thoroughly that she required a wheelchair for months. I never once acknowledged it. I refused to help her, pretending I couldn't hear her if she asked for a glass of water, walking at top speed to punish her for being so slow. She knew that my anger grew from my fear that she had let things fall apart, so she let me seethe. It was the way we both preferred it.

As far as sex was concerned, Qing acknowledged only the practical consequences and never the act itself. "So *when* you get pregnant," she told me before I left for college, as if we were already mid-discussion on this and my unwanted, forthcoming pregnancy were etched in stone, "you need to tell me so I come help you get an abortion." She wore open-backed dresses that were bandage-tight and often told me I looked nice in miniskirts and crop tops. But that's because, for her, the purpose of clothes was not to attract attention from men. Fashion was a totally sexless game strictly for those who took the same egg-headed interest in runway trends that others might take in bird-watching. This type of ignorance to *sexiness* was different from being prudish or conservative about the morality of sex, in which she seemed to place no stock. She was thrilled, for example, when my boyfriend and I moved in with each other—because of the money we'd save. The guiding principle was not to *stop* sex. It was simply to never acknowledge it.

And so we didn't.

I figured that Qing's enthusiasm about *Magic Mike XXL* was a more elaborate version of this tiptoeing we did. I tried to call her bluff: Would she be interested in seeing the live show in Vegas that Tatum was producing? She would say no, I expected—of course she would say no. *Magic Mike XXL* is a movie about strippers stripping; naturally, this live show would be of men, stripping.

I almost choked when she said yes, and nonchalantly suggested April for our trip.

I WOULD attempt to defang this experience the way I approached many things in my life—by taking it on as a work assignment. By reporting it out, I figured, I'd sand down the edges of the experience before it even happened, peek around every corner, get pre-accustomed to every potentially cringey moment. So I pitched a Mother's Day feature to my editor at *Refinery29* for a content package about motherhood as an adventure story and about how a new batch of male revues like *Magic Mike Live* were employing the language and hallmarks of feminism to entertain large groups of straight women—a concept so purehearted you could even take your mom!

I admit that I came up with the thesis before talking to a single interviewee, as a sort of desperate wish fulfillment. I hoped—wǒde mā ya I hoped—that I was right. The show's format seemed to support my hypothesis. Instead of your typical male stripper fantasy—the police officer knocking at the door of a bachelorette party, the construction worker who got too hot to continue hammering with clothes on, the slick socialite with a bow tie around his neck (and another one, as it usually turns out, around his penis)—*Magic Mike Live*, just like the movie, provided no elaborate backstory about why the abs had to come out. The abs were out because these men were not actually cops or roofers. They were out because this was a show about exemplary male bodies and all they can do. The dancing, I was informed over and over, was the entertainment being offered—not the "acting," the "fantasy." The tone they were trying to convey was one of empowerment, not titillation.

This was not an expansion of sex work; rather, *Magic Mike Live* was an innovation on *choreography*. All right!

I boarded the flight to Las Vegas with the kind of peace that comes only from the reassurance you get when you've thoroughly deluded yourself, and I met Qing at the terminal. Upon landing, we took a taxi to the hotel we had booked using extra time-share points—we dodged the salesperson at the front desk, unplugged the landline in the room, dodged the same salesperson again on the way out, and took the shuttle bus to the main Vegas strip half a mile away.

Qing had been to Las Vegas a handful of times in the past—once, when my sister and I were children on one of our road trips, staying at the only kid-friendly hotel on the strip, Circus Circus, which hadn't yet fallen into the grim state it's in now. That first trip was fine—it was convenient to find cheap places to eat, no one got bored, we kids didn't see any "bad things" except for a pair of bare ass cheeks on two women in sparkling thongs advertising a showgirls revue— but Vegas left a lasting impression on Qing, who'd return every few years, waiting for the day when her circumstances were finally such that she could accept what Vegas offered.

If a person has traveled at all, chances are they have traveled to Las Vegas. If you drive there, arriving at Las Vegas will feel like science fiction—it will emerge from the desert dunes like an oasis made of pure energy. If you fly, Vegas will announce itself while you're still emerging from the jetway, the sound of airport slot machines and the smell of indoor cigarette smoke a spiritual red carpet. Everything begs for your attention, your company, your money. With so much competition, everything from the architecture to the club promoters pull from the Earth's most recognizable enchantments: castles and pyramids, queens and whores, race cars, tigers, birds of paradise, the beach, the Eiffel Tower, voodoo, Elvis, murder, guns, chocolate. The effect is pure chaos and a context collapse. Standing on the corner of where our rideshare dropped us off, Qing and I could spot, without moving, the largest Buca di Beppo Italian chain restaurant we'd ever seen underneath the turrets of a concrete Camelot, a three-story-tall golden lion next to a video screen advertising a Lil Jon DJ set, a scaled-down Statue of Liberty *and* Empire State Building, and one roller coaster with no one on it.

One rule of excess is, with so much to look at, there's also so much to ignore. There is, like it's advertised, something for everyone. And in Vegas, where every door is understood to be a portal to an adventure, and every person is there because they're looking for a release, that goes for you, too. Anyone can be invisible if they're standing next to a person dressed only in feathers and rhinestones. And when you're invisible, you can do whatever you want.

Qing was drawn toward the liberation that Vegas demanded of its visitors: Have fun, let loose, break the rules, drink those free drinks, buy the expensive shoes. But the absolution waiting at the end was even more alluring. *What happens in Vegas stays in Vegas.* It was written on every event flyer, tourist brochure, and billboard. Vegas was a place without consequences, at least for the kind of meek peccadillos—ordering two desserts instead of dinner, staying up past midnight, wearing a lipstick color that was not mauve—that Qing considered to be her most extreme "bad" behavior.

There was the not-insignificant chance that the two of us would get into actual trouble. After circling the globe for documentary work and playing witness to how people act when they're on their best behavior, and then what they do when the cameras switch off, I believe there's a powerful correlation between the degree to which people wild out and the degree to which they feel the need to repress their feelings. The most polite, people-pleasing individuals are the ones who are carried home first from a party. Societies with the strictest rules regarding propriety and etiquette are the ones that have to have subway cars separating gropers from gropees. It will always be the salaryman who spends his life grinding himself down at the behest of those more powerful than him who will drink himself to nakedness during happy hour. It is always the Catholic school girls who will lose their virginities the first week of college. Always the teacher's pet who is the first to pass out at the graduation rager.

But we both had separate amulets that'd protect us from

the kind of debauchery only badly repressed people like ourselves are capable of. Qing was—and is—allergic to alcohol. A single sip of wine will blanket her in a rash, give her a migraine, and skyrocket her heart rate to that of a hamster's. Mine was a severe case of nausea that I hadn't yet realized was acid reflux. I knew that eating made it better and then much, much worse—and drinking anything other than water made me feel as if my entire gastrointestinal tract was radioactive. Plying myself with drinks would do more harm than good, and I tried not to think too much about what that meant.

Egged on by the show we had booked for *Magic Mike Live* on Saturday evening, slowed down by my guts and work obligations, we toed the line between impulse and structure. We walked through the grand atriums of the Bellagio as we had done before, trying not to be so obvious as we admired the glossy, pretty things in the high-end shop windows in the matter-of-fact way we were accustomed to. Look—don't touch—and absolutely do not go in.

But as we lingered outside the windows of Céline—the French luxury brand whose handbags were the designer bags of that moment—I found myself feeling emboldened: "Mom—let's go in."

Qing responded casually—"En," the Mandarin equivalent of *uh-huh*—and we swung right and walked through the doors.

Luxury retail is a terrifying experience. There is nothing similar, accessible to regular people, that engenders the same intense feelings of inadequacy, elation, shame, and desire—except perhaps for gambling. It turns the exchange of money into a spectator sport, where you, the shopper, are as much on display as the products for sale. Even the lighting subjects you to surveillance, drowning you in the kind of bright overhead glare that magics cocktail rings into pocket-sized solar systems and highlights every fiber of polyester in fluorescence. With all eyes on you, how do you convincingly suggest you're there for a legitimate reason—and not just to gape?

In my years as a fashion editor, I had learned small ways to slide into not being noticed. "Thanks—just browsing!" does not work (you might as well say "No thank you, I'll just be muttering at the price tags!" with your pockets turned inside out). Pretending that you're interested in buying something when you cannot will fool no one. Walking around with your hands behind your back, like you're strolling through some museum, will allow you a glimpse, but be entirely unsatisfying, as looking without touching is like smelling a cake you cannot eat. The only solution to all that, as I've workshopped, is to be honest about why you're there: because you want to hold and dote on the things you've only seen in photos.

Inside the Céline store, the majority of shoppers were handling its most popular handbags of the moment: the Luggage and the Trapeze, all sharp angles and gently curving trim, big enough for a small laptop but still meant to be carried in the crook of your arm, supple leather in muted tones. A salesperson immediately materialized: "Are you looking for something in particular?"

I smiled, remembering my lines. "Yes—but we're in no rush." I looped my arm through Qing's. The associate gave me a knowing nod and then retreated to help another customer.

And so we were left alone. I walked Qing over to the clothes I had seen in online slideshows of the Paris fashion shows—the long, fluid skirts that undulated like the glossy surface of a hotel pool, the heeled sandals that affixed to your feet by just an ankle strap and a loop for your big toe, the luscious leather pieces that felt like lotion in our hands. But what I really wanted to see in person was a color— International Klein Blue, to be exact—a brilliant cobalt made famous by the French pop artist Yves Klein. Céline's designer at the time, Phoebe Philo, had referenced the artist in her latest collection by dipping the hems of white cotton-poplin dresses in the hue and drenching a flannel-lined pair of trousers in it. From my computer screen, the color glowed a little brighter than the other pixels surrounding it, but in person, underneath the retail lighting, the blue beamed like it was alive. In the store, I stopped in front of the collection's most popular piece—a funnel-necked shift dress that had been stamped with a voluptuous human body dipped in blue, an homage to Yves Klein's *Anthropométries*, in which he used the body as a paintbrush. On the Céline dress, the body imprint broke out of two dimensions, broke out of three dimensions, and became a human with a story: There were lopsided breasts, a full belly, and vaselike thighs that curved forward, outward, and inward. "It's real?" Qing asked. I didn't know. Is it a copy? An original? Was there a real person who laid their real body against this dress? "Does it matter? It looks real." It was not a print of a horizontal body at rest—the gravity of where it pulled things down, the alignment of the parts, the contours of the strokes, was of a naked body standing in front of someone else, in a controlled, deliberate, wanted embrace. It was choreography. And up until that point, it was the sexiest thing I had ever seen in Vegas.

FOR THE REST of that day, we gently egged each other on to do the things that had always been just outside our comfort zone, just to see if we had it in us, and to pretend things had always been that way. Qing graciously accepted compliments without grimacing and made spicy little comments through the day that I pretended didn't shock me. A cab we had taken was pulled over for driving five miles above the speed limit, and after the traffic cop wrote us a ticket and handed it to our driver, Qing shrieked from the back seat: "You know why you got ticket?"

"Girl—" the driver started. I began to turn around, my eyes pleading that she not deliver a lecture about safety.

"Because we are *color people!*" Qing asserted, folding her hands and leaning back into her seat. The driver whooped in agreement, and they spent the rest of the trip telling each other about the speeding tickets they had unfairly gotten.

Back in the hotel room, getting ready for that evening, Qing walked into the bathroom, where I was finishing putting on my makeup. We had both decided on our outfits the week prior and agreed to coordinate—a lace top for me and a silk button-down for Qing, heels, and matching skinny jeans instead of skirts. We'd both wear bold lips. Dressed and nearly ready, I was in the middle of painting on a precise coat of long-wear lip stain the color of black cherries when Qing came in.

"Gòule ma?" she inquired: *Is this enough?* She was holding on to a thick stack of creaseless dollar bills. "Two hundreds."

I blinked.

"This is for throwing," she proceeded. "Right? Connie. For tip?"

"Y-yes!" I stammered, snapping back into form. "This— *that's right*. That's right. Where did you—did you go to the bank? *Mom!*"

As it turns out, I was not right. As part of the mainstreamification of the male revue, *Magic Mike Live* offered "unicorn dollars" to all ticket holders, pink rectangles of printer paper stamped with hearts and the words "You're Welcome." *Thank you*, I said to the Channing Tatum in my head, grateful that the evening was starting like a school carnival—a sign, I hoped, that what was to come was also PG.

As far as I could tell, we were not the only mother-daughter duo there. There were others like us; groups of gay men, too; some couples. The majority of the audience consisted of gaggles of women in coordinating outfits with sashes around their torsos and plastic veils on their heads, women who were obligated to have a wild weekend and approached this duty with various degrees of commitment. The decor was unintentionally kitschy; part strip-mall speakeasy, part magician's club, where you're likely to see someone wearing suspenders with a porkpie hat and novelty socks. The welcome music was somewhere between what you'd hear at a bat mitzvah and a club for mostly thirtysomethings. In the gift shop, there were books by Naomi Wolf for sale alongside egg-shaped rose-quartz orbs meant to tone your vaginal muscles. By the time the lights dimmed, I was almost relaxed. This place was clumsy, try-hard, inauthentic—a gibberish salad of references, genres, and aesthetics. I knew this place.

I don't want to spoil it for you, but *Magic Mike Live* is a good time. The jokes are self-aware ("You're in great and multicultural hands," the MC said about their hunk lineup). You never feel sorry for anyone—there are no exhausted dancers onstage, or brides-to-be getting forcibly dry-humped for laughs. And there are moments of true exhilaration. The dancers are athletes and artists, and the routines, whether choreographed or improvised, are appreciated by people who can't help but feel moved when watching human bodies masterfully negotiate strength and grace.

Plus, there was all the flinging about of "us" "showgoers," who I assumed *must be* hired actors because of how unwieldy the routines would have been if both parties hadn't practiced them first. Dozens of "ordinary women" around me got the Magic Mike treatment—they were flung, spun, and flipped like precious pancakes, making it through without injury to body or reputation. *What a diverse group of hired actors*, I noticed, pleased. I was impressed by the show's commitment to the idea that every woman was worthy of Magic Men. They were all ages, ethnicities, body types—the only thing connecting them was that they were all wearing pants. *Even that old lady over there*; I watched as a woman with gray hair was hoisted in the air while she was still seated, turned upside down, and then gently dragged along the floor. *What a fun acting gig*, I thought. *Good for you!*

I felt something on my shoulder. I looked at it. Whatever it was—logically, it must be a hand—was enormous, like a hot water bottle attached to five hot dogs. *Those fingers have muscles*, I remember thinking. They gripped my shoulder like it was a cheap paperback. *How funny*, my brain went. *They mistook me for one of the actors.*

"Will you join Ryan on the stage?"

Without thinking, I put my pocket-sized hand inside the god's hand, and felt myself switch into autopilot, my feet moving without being asked to, right up to the side of the stage, where my escort matter-of-factly ran down the safety tips: "Do not try to turn around and interact with Ryan. If you feel yourself slipping, it's okay to hold on. But keep your arms and legs inward so you don't accidentally get hit during the drum solo."

"I'm sorry, what—drum solo?—"

If you have never sat on someone's lap, backward, as they are performing a drum solo in front of a live audience— please, let me explain it to you. It is like sitting in the backward-facing seat in the last row of an ancient wagon on a country road. It is jarringly bumpy, and a little lonely. You have a view that no one else has, except you have the sneaking suspicion that everyone else's view is better than yours. Because you can't really see much of anything, including much of Ryan or much of yourself except for your high-heeled right foot that is gently jostling in the air, like a baby's foot in a high chair. Under the hot stage lights, you can barely make out the crowd, either—and besides, they're moving too much, a mass of pumping arms and open mouths.

The only thing that will be visible will be your mother's face, because, unlike everything else, it will not be moving, because she will be singularly focused on the glowing screen of her iPhone as she tapes the encounter with the determined, proud focus of a stage mom.

And afterward, if your experience is similar to how mine was, your mother will come up to you with a big hug. "I film you," she will say. And you will flush with mortification—but not shame—and tell her to never show anyone, least of all yourself. And even though you know you will never watch the video, you will be glad it exists. It will be an experience you had once dreaded and feared. But you'll realize that after all has been said and done, the real secret to neutralizing bad things is to stare them right in the eye.

# SIX

# Fancy Things
## *Versailles*

L ike most other suburban build-a-homes, the closet inside my parents' place was a major selling point. It's called a walk-in, but that isn't exactly fair to all the closets that qualify as such. By then, we had lived in many apartments with closets that landlords would boast as "walk-ins"—a converted hallway with rods that led to the only bathroom in the space, or a regular closet, just one awkward foot too deep. On TV, a reporter once interviewed a teenage Tara Lipinski, who showed off the twin mattress on the floor of the "walk-in" she slept in so she and her mother could live closer to the training rink.

But my parents' closet lived up to the promise of luxury. Ten feet by ten feet, with layers of rubber-coated white rail shelving encircling three and a half walls, their closet—bigger than some of the bedrooms in our past apartments—was vast enough to waltz in. My dad's clothes took up maybe two feet of one rod, roomy jeans and zipped sweatshirts, faux-aged graphic shirts that had eventually become actually aged screen printed with rock clubs that didn't exist or boasting hometown pride from cities we'd only driven through. My mother's clothes took up the rest of the space. Categorized maniacally, hung scrupulously, packed away in neat garbage bags or in bound-up suitcases, her clothes were treated like jewels. Qing never got rid of any clothing if she had loved it, so it was all there—the first pair of stonewashed jeans she bought on the black market in China, the silk sundresses I never saw her wear except in photos, the almond-toe pumps that were so old and cheaply made they cracked like tiny knuckles when I'd step into them.

If you bought one of these McMansions, you could pick from a full suite of these types of novelty luxuries, like intercom systems and built-in wet bars. One of my friends in the neighborhood had a cedar-lined sauna, never used, that we kids had commandeered as a clubhouse. My parents had declined most of these add-ons except for the ones their salesperson told them were essential to the home's resale potential, like the dishwasher they still use only to store everyday dishes, or the gas fireplace no one remembers how to turn on. But my mom was adamant that they splurge for the nice closet. Looking at her clothes and rearranging them had always been her hobby, she told us. More than that, I came to understand, the closet was the only place she knew to go to calm herself down. After an outburst of anger, she'd move her necklaces from one surface to another, refold her jeans so the towers were exactly the same width, until her jaw stopped tingling.

After my sister and I left home, my mother's apparel footprint grew. Swallowing both our bedrooms and its closets, the guest room, the hall closets, and the kitchen pantry, her wardrobe expanded into wings—a separate space for her bags, her jewelry, her shoes, and her dresses. On Sundays, she walks from room to room, paying respects to her collection of smart shift dresses she got on sale from Ann Taylor, the clutches of costume jewelry laid out on paper towels that cover the same desks we once did homework on, the Chanel bag she bought in New York City that she's taken out to admire more often than she's taken out to carry. After being reimagined as Qing's fashion palace, the home that was once too big for the four of us became just right for her.

I know that my love of fashion was born out of Qing's. Shopping was one of the few times when she'd be generous with me as a teenager, encouraging me to experiment and explore. She would rationalize saying yes to buying clothes the same way she'd rationalize saying no to staying out past curfew. We subscribed to fashion magazines, purchased with airline points, that I'd read in peace, knowing that while I had one of these magazines in hand, she'd never badger me about whether I had done another practice SAT exam. Fashion was a medium I revered as a fantasy and an escape, a way to be comfortable cosplaying as a thing before actually embarking on the thing itself, or abandoning it if it didn't, quite literally, fit: a punk in high school; a hipster in college; someone who appeared to understand art, drugs, literature, and sex. Sometimes I was too good at being a poseur, finding myself in embarrassing situations where I'd be forced to reveal just how superficial my charade actually was. But in the process, I grew to understand the vernacular of fashion and the superpower it had to communicate anything I wanted. Especially in phases where I felt silent and weak, I turned to fashion in order to yell.

It was a theme I tried to explore as a fashion editor. In some ways, I saw my work as something similar to a language teacher, instructing women in how to communicate, to express their interior lives. Among the dozen articles I'd publish a day, most were simple lessons in grammar and vocabulary: ways to tuck in a shirt, match your prints, and shop for jeans. And then, occasionally, I'd put all the pieces together by translating the stories that women—from the fancy to the ordinary, the privileged to the marginalized—were telling through their clothing.

Fashion is semiotics; a communication device, something to be studied, cataloged, critiqued, and wielded. But fashion is also a carnal pleasure in a way that fine art cannot be. It is a sense-shaker, a treat for your eyes, nose, skin, and ears. It physically attaches itself to you, bearing down on your shoulders and grazing your skin, constantly reminding you that it is there, and that you like that it is there. A good meal lasts two or three hours, tops. A grand vista lasts as long as you are willing to be present to observe it. But the pleasure of a good outfit will last all day, and continue to deliver every time it's worn.

As part of my job, I attended Fashion Week—four of them, some lasting up to ten days and one as short as five, twice every year. Nearly every region has its own, from Omaha to Osaka, but it's New York City, London, Milan, and Paris that host the designers and collections that constitute what most within the establishment would define as *the* establishment. It is Chanel, Burberry, and Gucci; it is *Vogue* and its lineup of tidy editors in chief—one of each from every continental market, the American Girl dolls of global fashion. It's department store buyers and critics from the same four newspapers dressed in all black. Of course, there are small waves of change, trends in how Fashion

Week is conducted, like when social media influencers entered the fray, or when Chinese billionaires replaced Dallas billionaires in the front row. Once, Georgia, the country, became extremely relevant. But what has been everlasting is the thinness and the whiteness at the center of fashion, and the idea that the kind of exclusivity those principles demand is valuable, normal, and good.

At face value, Fashion Week is a simple concept: It is a convention where designers sell their clothing to stores, during which those in the media can witness these commercial transactions in order to advance, critique, or glom on to the business being conducted. It—in theory—should be no different than a trade show filled with booths and vendors. And at times in history, this was the case. But during the years in which I attended shows, the pageantry of Fashion Week often required more money to pull off than it had the potential to pull in. It became its own cultural phenomenon, with strict hierarchies and an elite class that demanded a unique set of customs and protocol. Navigating it engendered a social experience as hypnotic and intense as finding yourself in a foreign country.

As such, attending the international parts of Fashion Week is a travel experience unlike anything else. It is equal parts pleasure and pain, especially if you are not among the front-row elite. As a mid-tier editor from a mid-tier digital publication, I was definitely on the outside, but I belonged enough to be allowed to peer inward. I was physically there, listening to the same soundtrack and blinking under the same lights as Tim Blanks or Emmanuelle Alt—but from my seat, I rarely got to see anything below models' hips. I was invited to attend parties, but not dinners. Publicists would return most of my emails, as long as I played nicely— and I would know based on where I was seated if they felt that I had not. Once, before a show began, I attempted to get a quote from Anna Wintour for an article I was working on: Rebuffed by her security and spotted by the publicists organizing the event, my seat was pushed to the back row the following season. Sometimes, I wouldn't get a seat at all after a negative review, which meant I had earned a spot on designers' blacklists—Dolce & Gabbana; Jeremy Scott; Victoria's Secret, right before the Ed Razek era ended— from which publicists expected me to grovel my way off.

I want to make it clear: I did not think I belonged in the front row. I had no real business that required that vantage point! For the most part, I did not take these things personally. But it grated to be told *you are exactly this important* two dozen times a day. Even a cotton ball can make you bleed if it rubs you long enough. We were fueled on all sorts of uppers through the day and evening, and then powered down with a strong sleeping pill around 2:00 a.m., after all the day's stories were filed, to bludgeon ourselves through the jet lag. The constant micro-slights and the intense, repetitive structure—a show every hour for twelve hours for fifty days in a row—can be destructive. I have seen mentally fit women throw tantrums after receiving a rejection to a show after a long day; I've witnessed fashion editors charge thousands of dollars of money they don't have to their credit cards in order to buy clothing they can't wear anywhere but to fashion shows, all to fight against the feeling of spiraling backward. Once, a colleague, in a morass of self-loathing and self-delusion, reacted with psychotic glee to a Parisian Uber driver who leaned out the window of the car to call out her name, the one he read from the app: "Yes, it's me! It's me!" she cried, clutching her chest. "How wonderful! Did you recognize me from street-style photos?"

Through it all, most maddeningly, we understood that these were champagne problems at their fizziest. We knew what it sounded like to complain about going to fashion shows. We knew how stupid it was to complain about being in Paris. It turns out that the hate we had for it all laid a pretty cozy foundation for the hate we began to develop for ourselves. The point of it all, I kept telling myself, is to have a clear vision of the bottom line, the center, the status quo. *I am here to witness, not to participate*, I'd repeat ineffectually, like a mantra, tasting salt.

I never complained directly to Qing, of course—I knew better than that—but I also stopped gushing about the trips after I returned during our phone calls. "My big regret," she said to me once, unprompted, after a particularly tedious season, "is when I retire, you will stop to go to Fashion Weeks. When will I go to Paris?"

I thought about Qing in her closet, flipping through the clothes she had bought on sale in the mall, worshipping these watered-down imitations of the fashion I saw, and whined about, in person. I looked up flights that night.

UNTIL THEN, Qing had technically traveled to only one continent, North America. Before then, there had been no opportunities: Private Chinese citizens weren't allowed the privilege to travel legally outside the country, never mind having the funds to pay for it. My mom's father, whose calculated discretion and diplomatic instincts eventually got him promoted from working at a publishing house to an important job as a state minister, had once taken a business trip to Japan, where he tried to buy my mom a dress as a souvenir, only to discover that they all cost more than his monthly paycheck.

Having ventured into only English-speaking Canadian provinces and tourist-trap resorts in Mexico, this would be a first. The trip would take us through London, Paris, and Rome, a greatest-hits tour that would finally bring Qing to all the European destinations she had read about in novels and seen in black-and-white pictures of women smoking cigarettes in fascinating clothes against decaying back-drops: Buckingham Palace, Notre-Dame, the Colosseum . . . We'd go to places where we could get dressed up and see fine things in person. With only three days in each city, our consumption would be fast and furious, a smash-and-grab affair that would hopefully leave us delirious and de-pleted, but in the happy sort of way.

We'd need to travel light but look acceptable for a sweeping range of foreign environments in which what you wore determined how little you would be bothered. We'd be on our feet all day, but walking shoes—worn with walking clothes—would be a missed opportunity for fashion moments. The weather, too, would be inconsistent: European springtime brought about chaos in which rain, frost, heat waves, and perfect weather were all equal pos-sibilities.

This was exactly the kind of trip I excel at when it comes to what to pack. I had always been a daydream plan-ner since those early road trips, agonizing over outfit com-binations with an unyielding discipline to two masters: economy of space and maximal style. (In college, when I first encountered Joan Didion along with the rest of the women in my dorm, it was her packing list—not her descriptions of naivete and youth, of counterculture, of self-respect—that got me hooked. Here was a woman who knew the power of the contents of a suitcase, who was not afraid to rewear the same piece many times, who planned for and looked forward to discomfort, who understood that a skirt and flat shoes were like an invisibility cloak. I remember thinking that I could not have dinner with her or hold a conversation with her, but I could certainly travel with her.)

I had my own qualifications. Every Fashion Week required full-peacocking looks without obvious overlapping of items (but given the small rooms we stayed in, everything had to fit in one checked suitcase and one carry-on), and I had gotten more efficient with every season, eventually reaching a point where I never brought a single thing I didn't wear and never had to scramble to dash into an H&M to find something I had forgotten at home. Once, I spent a month on the road during a sabbatical from work, and I fit everything for a five-country tour into one hard-shell carry-on. When I was filming *Style Out There*, I was limited to two outfits per episode despite the number of days we were to film, which actually helped things; I circumnavigated the globe with one large suitcase on wheels that I checked, and one tiny carry-on that contained only what I immediately needed for the next leg; at the end of each shoot, I'd rearrange the contents of my suitcase in case the big one got lost in transit.

This is all to say that I am very good at packing, mostly because I adhere to the following commandments:

- Nearly every top should match with nearly every bottom.
- Expect to rewear every item constantly, but strive to make each outfit unique.
- No matter what, never bring more than three pairs of shoes.
- Leave at least a third of the suitcase empty for souvenirs.
- Err on the side of conservatism—always have a way to cover your shoulders, upper thighs, arms, and head.*

I had even, at one point, come up with a convoluted formula to calculate how many tops and bottoms and one-pieces I would need based on the number of days the trip would require and the number of permutations the items made possible. I've shared versions of this packing list with friends and colleagues, who have always seemed more interested in the

---

*I realized the importance of the last one by trial and error. I've always liked to dress modestly (not for any moral reasons—it's purely an aesthetic preference), but my blousy tops and cutoff shorts still made me look like a cultural terrorist at the front gates of Wat Rong Khun temple in Chiang Rai, or to see *The Last Supper* in Milan. While queuing in Delhi to see the Jama Masjid mosque, I thought I was clever by wearing my airplane stole—an oversized silk scarf patterned in a bandanna paisley—around my head, like a toddler with their blankie. I might have technically adhered to the dress code, but I looked like I was messing with them. The guard begrudgingly ushered me in after giving me a displeased up-and-down. My personal discomfort at how ridiculous I looked in such a nonridiculous space was overwhelming. As soon as I entered, I made a quick beeline for the exit and ejected myself.

philosophy than in the actual practice. But on the off-chance that this will be helpful to a chronic over- or under-packer, here is my personal packing list:

- A small number of basic tops that are nice but not formal. Striped oxfords, your favorite T-shirts, and a ribbed turtleneck all qualify.
- A smaller number of charming bottoms that are un-fussy in fabric, like a dramatic pair of denim, a flounce wrap skirt in a wrinkle and stain-resistant fabric, or a pair of flared corduroy trousers.
- A thin outer layer (depending on the climate, I usu-ally go for a black cardigan or a lightweight Uniqlo Heattech puffer jacket that squishes down into the size of a fist).
- A single uncrushable dress (Issey Miyake Pleats Please is a personal favorite).
- Given chillier weather, two substantial outer layers: one long and one short, making sure that one of them is slightly fancier than the other. I like a mack-intosh in a swishy, wipeable fabric and a barn coat; or an oversized teddy-bear shearling and a leather jacket.
- Two to three pairs of reliable broken-in shoes, includ-ing party sneakers, thusly named because you wouldn't be embarrassed to wear them to a casual party (my go-tos are Air Max 97s) and nice but neutral flats. Optional: a practical but audacious pair of heels to level up a semi-nice outfit into a really nice one.
- A small cross-body bag for daily essentials, a nice canvas tote for occasional schlepping, and a soft clutch to use as a pouch for electronics or toiletries (until you need it to be a clutch).

- No more underwear than you think you need (you can always buy more from the drugstore, in a pinch), one bra, three pairs of socks, and one set of pajamas.
- A swimsuit, a large scarf or shawl, a pair of sunglasses, and one flashy pair of earrings.
- A soft outfit (matching sweats, a big sweater, and thick leggings) that you should wear on planes and trains, as soon as you return from a long day out, or for past-midnight lounging by the hotel bar (with heels and earrings, if the vibe necessitates it).
- Makeup in stick form, skincare decanted into small jars and tubes, eyeglasses and 10 percent more pairs of contacts than you think you might need, and an old-fashioned toothbrush and American toothpaste.
- Chargers (but no electronics other than a phone and an external battery for it).

Save for truly extraordinary circumstances (a black-tie gala, a days-long camping excursion, going to Mars), packing this way works for nearly all manner of countries and cultures. It gives you the best shot of being able to walk five miles to have aperitifs at a Michelin restaurant and tour the Colosseum right afterward. It allows for luggage space to bring home bulky treasures, but the approach is not so spartan that you have to wear the same outfit each time the sun goes down. It has served me well, and I only wished I had warned Qing about its virtues before we left for Europe.

WE STARTED off aggressively, logging 29,000 steps the first day. Qing had prepared a great set of practical outfits to wear in London: a striped oxford shirt with a calf-length leather skirt, a gray shift dress over a silk turtleneck, and a yellow space-knit sweater dress—all worn with a new pair of designer sneakers she had just bought at the outlet mall. "They're comfortable," she insisted, as she covered the blisters already sprouting by her toes with bandages, the super-adhesive kind that, I warned her, you're supposed to leave on for days in order for the blisters to dry up and heal. After the bandages went on, we walked an hour from Holborn to Shoreditch during magic hour, one of the first warm evenings that year, the streets teeming with people in business casual, vibrating at the thrill of being outdoors after a long winter. She was limping by the time we got to the restaurant. Afterward, when we stood up to leave, I saw her breath catch in her throat as she put weight on her feet. We took a cab home.

For the next couple of nights while I slept, Qing, disgusted at the idea of trapped sweat and dirty feet, would remove the bandages you weren't supposed to remove. Each morning when we left the hotel, ignorant of her clandestine activities, I'd tell her that we'd take it easy, that she'd probably feel better the next day, to let the bandages do their job. On the morning of our last day in London, she revealed what she had been doing. She sat on the edge of the toilet, frowning at the oozing craters on her feet. "How can I sleep without washing first?" she said, wincing. She hadn't brought any other shoes that wouldn't rub in those exact spots, except for a pair of canvas flip-flops that she had originally planned on wearing around our hotel rooms like house slippers.

And so Qing arrived in chilly Paris—her fashion mecca—wearing what was almost nearly her most capable outfit: a polka-dot dress with sheer balloon sleeves, a chic red box bag covered in blue bonbon buttons, giant bug-eye sunglasses . . . and those flip-flops. "Don't look at them," she'd moan, as I leaned against her in line at the Eiffel Tower. "So embarrassed!" she cried as they slapped against the marble steps in the Louvre, echoing like a whip crack. Her feet were red from the cold, and the flip-flops were slow and slippery. But impracticality wasn't the shoes' real crime. "Even the American tourists don't wear them here," she whispered in a panic as we joined the others walking along the Avenue de Paris to Versailles at dawn.

It was something that she had been commenting on since we arrived, how you could always spot an American tourist in the crowd. American tourists dressed, as she put it, exactly like their children—short jackets in stain-proof fabrics, running sneakers and baseball hats, the men in shorts with either a surfeit of cargo pockets or no pockets at all, and the women in stretch-denim or patterned leggings. Even from a distance, you could spot Americans by the colors they chose. Tourists from the rest of the world mostly kept to staid neutrals, conservative patterns, and deep jewel tones—even the flashy ones, in skintight denim that'd been whiskered to death or florid tracksuits that matched their knockoff Gucci trainers, mostly wandered the streets in muted, anodyne shades. But American families abroad, from toddlers to grandparents, dressed in a palette of playground colors: magenta, teal, cotton candy, and sky blue, a multigenerational merry band of spandex-blend jersey. Most striking yet is that while other tourists err on the side of formal, Americans will always choose the more casual version.

One thing though about the Ugly American cliché: It's a stereotype that no longer actually exists. While it's easy to recognize Americans abroad by our aggressively practical, bright clothing, no one wears aloha shirts and fanny packs anymore, or leather sandals with white tube socks. The way the Ugly American behaves, loud and oblivious, peeing in bidets, ordering Bud Lights at brasseries, is also outdated. After a generation of educational travel programming and tempered by embarrassing presidents, Americans have, at the very least, learned how to keep their patriotism to themselves. I believe that standard American tourists also act how they dress: down-to-earth, without romance or pretension, but also there to please no one—no dress code—but themselves.

And the garment that best fulfills these qualities, weather permitting? Flip-flops.

Thawing London was full of American tourists in leather Rainbow sandals and bronze Jack Rogers. But Paris was cold. My mother was a lone flopper. The rest of her was dressed for Versailles, in a thick-striped sweater dress, a faux-crocodile handbag, a long pendant necklace, and a smart long-length coat with gold buttons. But her bare feet were a sartorial record-scratch—an aberration that betrayed the intentionality she put into the rest of the look. Her mood was ruined.

Upon crossing the last boulevard, the bottle-green roofs of Versailles within spitting distance, we somehow made a wrong turn and ended up in the parking lot for bus tours. We were surrounded by a hundred caravans neatly parked in a tight chevron configuration, with dozens of new ones pulling in while dozens pulled out with mesmerizing efficiency. And nearly all of them carried Chinese tourists. Bedecked in all sorts of competing colors, clashing patterns, and fabrics you normally wouldn't see outside of a New Year's Eve party—spangly sequins, vibrant stretch-satin, lace, mohair, and Lycra—they traveled in packs chasing after a tour guide, two dozen formal hats and frilly parasols following a single raised pennant. Similar to Americans, the way mainland Chinese tourists dressed also existed in a vacuum, ignoring norms and decorum, and oftentimes Western trends, too. But unlike Americans, they dressed with pure exuberance and enthusiasm, each a bigger show-off than the last.

The effect was totally bizarre, like seeing a birthday cake in the middle of the forest. All the more so because before I graduated from high school, I had never once encountered a mainland Chinese tourist outside of China. That was by design. It wasn't until 2005 that the Chinese Communist Party deregulated their travel restrictions—an important phase of their state tourism plan that was intended to ease the country into the consequences of introducing the world to its citizenry and its citizenry to the world, while maintaining firm political and economic control—finally allowing Chinese tourists to venture beyond a small list of approved destinations for reasons other than to visit friends and relatives. By that morning in Versailles, Chinese citizens had enjoyed thirteen years of nearly unfettered travel, and in that time, the business of tourism had become a super-machine, having now developed the infrastructure to satisfy millions of people.

For Chinese tourists, one of the clear benefits of traveling, especially to Europe, is to circumvent the country's high import taxes on anything foreign-made, including the fashion I saw each season during Fashion Week. Until recently, luxury clothing came with a 16 percent tariff, which disincentivized designers from selling within China. That meant that if you were a Chinese shopper who wanted to buy a Chanel flap bag, you'd have fewer options, more competition from other shoppers, fewer assurances it's not a knockoff, and—ultimately—would have to pay nearly two thousand dollars more than if you were to buy it in Paris. Many have figured that it makes more dollar-sense to shop abroad. When Qing and I were in Versailles, shopping-as-tourism was a giant subsection of outbound Chinese travel, cementing Chinese tourists in the top spot in total tourism spending, dropping $1.2 billion more annually than the second-highest spenders, Americans, despite representing only a small fraction of total global travelers. According to prepandemic figures, Chinese tourists accounted for half of luxury brand sales worldwide, with 85 percent of them made in Western countries.

Naturally, Western brands immediately understood them to be a gargantuan market opportunity, and set out to hire Chinese-speaking salespeople and work with tour guides to establish their stores as official stops on their itineraries. Along the way, these hacks took on an increasingly degrading and humiliating quality for Chinese shoppers, who were often allowed to enter stores only through the back or made to wait in long lines that non-Chinese shoppers could bypass. Stories about mistreatment and discriminatory practices flooded WeChat, warning Chinese shoppers where they'd be treated poorly. Online, "shopping while Chinese" is an experience many young Chinese tourists bemoan, though few understood how cringey a phrase it is to misappropriate, turning Black Americans' grievance of being pegged as criminals—assumed to have no money, mistreated because they could not possibly belong—to a lesser-stakes charge: being discriminated against for having money but no class.

This push and pull of being catered to, but without respect; of being familiar with the attractions and sights, but not the language; of wanting to experience the unfamiliar, but not get lost in it, leads many Chinese tourists to seek out group trips in order to dampen the blow. Though some Chinese citizens travel independently, a huge number naturally feel more comfortable signing up for a tour group. There are groups that cater to every type of Chinese tourist: those for whom Paris is a once-in-a-lifetime trip and would rather sleep at night on a bus if it means squeezing in another sightseeing opportunity; the social-media-obsessed tourist who can't say they've been to a place unless they took a selfie there; the family who wants to spend quality time together somewhere exotic and educational in order to enlighten Junior's mind and give the parents something to talk about later; the shopper who'd rather experience a place via the souvenirs they bring home; the novice traveler who doesn't speak or read English, thinks all white people look alike, and would much prefer starving than be forced to eat a bleeding steak and uncooked vegetables, but who's always wanted to see the Sun King's golden palace for themselves.

That morning, they were *all* at Versailles.

Qing slowed down to eavesdrop. The dialects and slang came from all over—north and south, cosmopolitan and country, old and young. Some were obviously rich. Some were much less so. Used to being the only Chinese person, not to mention the only Asian—sometimes the only non-white person—Qing found herself, in Paris, of all places, as part of the majority.

"*I can't believe this*," she said loudly in Chinese, then caught herself. We had always spoken in Mandarin when we had something private to say, always confident no one else could understand us. Here, we were safer speaking in English.

She recalibrated. "I never imagining Chinese people could come to here, and *so many*."

And then, "I am so proud."

She meant it. It had taken so much for her to come so far, and it meant something to see familiar faces once she arrived. They had taken divergent paths: she alone, them at the whims and mercy of the government—but they were all there now, together. There was another thing she sensed, too, standing among thousands of other Chinese speakers in the courtyard of a home built as a testament to having it all. She felt, for the first time outside of China, the ease that comes with not being a minority, of belonging without having to fight for it. Here, even in those flip-flops, she was invisible. And it felt good.

THE PALACE of Versailles has always been a tourist destination, even when it was the main residence of Louis XVI and Marie Antoinette, who allowed anyone who showed up in splendid enough clothes to enter its halls. Rich folks from as far as Southeast Asia traveled to Versailles to sightsee governing in action, from signing proclamations to hosting dinners. Stay long enough and you might even see the queen give birth! They also came to be entertained, fed, and enlightened. As the cultural center of Europe, Versailles was Fashion Week, Cannes Film Festival, Art Basel, South by Southwest, and Restaurant Week rolled into one. There, tourists came to see the latest fads and fashions, from classical music to gravity-defying hairdos, the latest mirror-making technologies (which were considered state secrets), massive ballets, and child chamber-music prodigies, as well as clothing and furniture made in the l'orientale style, inspired by Chinese diplomats and mimicking Chinese designs, but "refined" for Western tastes.

The buildings were objects of fashion themselves—the highlight being the Hall of Mirrors, a gilded gallery flanked by two walls of perfectly arched glass, like veneers in a mouth. It was a space not quite unlike my mother's closet, for admiring fashion. But here it took on a Midas quality, turning everything and everyone who entered *into* fashion, transforming each gesticulation, manner, relationship, and utterance into something to be gazed upon and coveted. The room turned subjects into objects, and objects into subjects, confusing governance and rule into an actual spectacle. As I gazed around, I realized that despite having traveled to Paris a half dozen times for Fashion Week, I had never bothered to visit Versailles, which would have given me the opportunity to be battered by the obvious allegory: Of course, this shrine to luxury, a distraction from urgent, fomenting trouble, could not and did not last. The French Revolution began at Versailles's golden gates.

The opulence was overwhelming, even for citizens of the twenty-first century. Beds were the size of rooms, murals stretched forever, gold was polished so intensely that it looked almost plastic. But the real exhibition was, once again, the people: hundreds of us fellow tourists crowded into arena-sized rooms, which began to feel as claustrophobic as Tara

Lipinski's "walk-in." The only place to look was up, and thankfully the Hall of Mirrors was stunning from that angle, with chrysanthemum-like crystal chandeliers sprouting from the ceiling every few feet, an inverted rain forest floor. The ceiling frescoes were beautiful, a heavenly cloudscape with the Sun King (I guessed, because I couldn't get close enough to any plaques to read about what I was looking at) gazing upward, surrounded by throbbing bodies, not unlike the scene below it, although the painted figures appeared much more serene.

Moving through the apartments was no better. There was literally no room or time to stop and look. People pushed against me from all sides, and I eventually gave up on trying to steer my body in any direction at all, surrendering to the tide of the crowd, hoping that the slow shuffling would eventually carry me outside. It was anarchy, made all the more surreal by the environment, which demanded silence, reverence. People were attempting to coordinate with one another, at the top of their lungs, like we were in an escape room; the signs requesting we turn off the flash on our phones and keep our arms behind the red ropes were about as visible and effective as a stop sign in a blizzard. In one of the bedrooms, a selfie stick found its way to the side of my face, and when I protested, the owner of it clucked her tongue in anger that I ruined her shot. *WHERE IS LINYUN?* a man next to me bellowed in Mandarin.

*LINYUN, ARE YOU IN THIS ROOM? (HERE, I AM HERE,* cried a voice from beyond.)

I found my mother in the courtyard, squinting at the sun in the sky, now directly overhead. "I have to pee," she said bleakly. I glanced over her shoulder to the line outside the bathroom—and the other not-quite line of Chinese tourists confidently strolling through the door, ignoring everyone else.

"Please!" a German woman cried in English. "There's a queue!" A sound emerged from the bathroom: *COME HERE, I AM INSIDE, I HAVE A TOILET FOR YOU.*

We decided to try our luck elsewhere, boarding a trolley to take us to Versailles's Hameau de la Reine, a miniature village that Marie Antoinette built for the amusement of herself and her girlfriends. There was a pond with an operational mill wheel and a still-working farm with animals. There was a boudoir, a farmhouse, a dairy, a grotto, and tiny cottages for which Antoinette had hired poor locals to pretend to be palatably poor villagers. For however extra the palace at Versailles was, this hamlet, a rich person's ode to the virtuousness of poverty, was—to me—the most sickeningly extravagant thing about the grounds.

For some reason, we were mostly alone. Not a single tour-bus tourist was there, probably because it was too far to visit before they had to hit the road again. To our relief, we found an empty restroom.

Afterward, I began pulling up articles to "Did you know . . ." the time away. It was a game I had begun playing on trips with Qing, a sort of bastard version of the homework I'd have to do as a child. Conversation-starters really, it involves pulling up unreliable news sources—the kinds of websites littered with chum-box advertisements selling belly-fat busters that also structures all articles as lists—that we'd take turns reading aloud to each other, discussing the credibility of these "facts." I rattled them off as we strolled through the gardens of the Petit Trianon: *Did you know that, as a member of the court, you could watch the king fall asleep every night as entertainment? Did you know that Louis XIV lost his virginity to a prostitute named "one-eyed Kate"? Did you know most of the food the royals ate was cold?*

And, most pertinently to us, *Did you know that there was a lack of toilets at Versailles, and so people just peed and pooped in hallways and behind curtains, including the Princesse d'Harcourt, who was famous for leaving a trail of waste behind her as she walked?*

We chuckled as we made our way back to the trolley. It was naive of us to think that fancy white people behaved any better than fancy Chinese people. But believing that, for Qing and me, was as reflexive as sneezing. In public, it was natural to behave, because it was natural to be scared of what would happen if we didn't. Fear of others' notice—"Do you see who's looking at you?"—was fundamental to our idea of being among people. But here, seeing those whose actions and clothing, the decibels of their voices even, demand attention and exception was like an unhealed blister forced opened and then washed clean. The shame that someone might mistake *me* as *them* gave way to a perverse kind of feeling. They *did not care*—about white history or white rules or white tourists in white lines. They traveled the world as elites in their own realities, caring about nothing except their own entertainment. And, as we later debated on the metro ride home, if you were going to be a real pill about authenticity and manners, and argue about how people ought to behave and how respect ought to be paid, those Chinese visitors were the only ones acting in the true spirit of Versailles—rude and crude, with empty bladders.

It wasn't a noble way to be, we knew that. But it had clearly once been a royal one.

At the train station, we found a cobbler attached to a small shoe shop that had just laid out their spring inventory. Qing left wearing a fun new pair of sandals with a rainbow platform and Velcro straps that did not bother her wounds. She liked them so much she continued to wear them for the rest of the trip, even when her blisters finally healed. She still wears them, in fact. And for the first time, I left Paris feeling healed, too. Again, I had seen the status quo: the exclusivity and entitlement, the emptiness masquerading as extravagance. But seeing it expressed with faces that looked like mine revealed it to be a farce. It's always been a joke, I realized, and I finally felt free enough of it to laugh.

# SEVEN

# R&R
## *Amsterdam*

Sleep came as elusively to Qing as it came easily to the rest of us, a family of snoozers who regularly slept until 11:00 a.m. on the weekends; who could doze on planes and in the back seats of cars; who considered it great fun to debate the advantages of a forty-five-minute nap versus a three-hour nap. Dexin, Julia, and I slept like people who've never lacked for it. To us, sleep was a daily treat that came naturally and effortlessly, never a source of stress or something that necessitated strategizing. But while we slept in and slept on, Qing did not sleep at all.

Her troubles began while she was in college and shared a dorm room with seven other students. Away from home for the first time, Qing found herself suddenly unable to shut off, staring into the baseboards of the bunk bed above her for hours on end, waiting for her thoughts to lose their sharpness, the kinetic energy in her limbs to uncoil, until the room began to be visible from the gray light leaking in, and it became late enough to reasonably be considered early, and okay for her to begin her morning.

During good nights, Qing sleeps for three hours. On bad nights she gets no sleep at all, but five hours of bedrest still does something—"If I pretend to sleeping, I can wake up with no headache." By 3:00 a.m., Qing is usually padding around the house setting things right, Swiffering the floors until they're buffed to a shine, prepping meals for the week, and reorganizing the cabinets and drawers to find even more efficient ways of arranging things. Bad sleepers like her, she often says with a sigh, have a shorter life expectancy. Might as well get something done with that extra time.

Qing has looked into every treatment available to her, from hard-core prescriptions and shock therapy to every Costco sleep aid offered through the years. She has tried meditation and mind management tactics and folk remedies that insomniacs trade like gossip. Once, her doctor prescribed for her the highest dosage of Ambien—double the recommended amount for women her size—which she swallowed over the kitchen sink, right before bed. When she woke up, she found herself splayed on the bottom of the carpeted stairs leading up to the second floor. The next morning, she answered my phone call sounding like her throat was wearing a sweater. "I still only sleep thirty minutes," she complained. After that, she made sure to take the pills only after she was already horizontal in bed, but even so, the Ambien would offer her only one violent hour of sleep, jostling her awake with the same brutality as when it knocked her out. She never refilled the prescription.

I've often wondered how it would feel to never be rested. I could only draw upon the rare instances when I've been jet-lagged or sleep-deprived by necessity, my brain suddenly taking on a perceivable physical mass, growing sour and hot, grinding to operate. Thinking is impossible for me in these conditions—even passively existing requires a noticeable expenditure of energy. Exhaustion logic is flip-flopped; it is much more arduous to be patient and calm, and much more comfortable to flail, storm, bark. But even with only half an hour of sleep, Qing says she feels "fine" and "clear," which, to me, seems to say more about relativism than it does the truth.

It was the summer of 2019, and no one I knew was sleeping particularly well. There was a general sense of ennui among my friends, many of whom felt like they had hit a wall. The daily, urgent acts of survival in New York had become routine. For some of us, it even became easy. Encounters with the novel and the bizarre struck us with less impact; the tsunami of rapture that used to bowl us over on the daily felt like little laps against our ankles, and it took a lot to even recognize those sensations. Big nights out—shots of well tequila for the table and Fernet with the bartenders; pressing our sweaty cheeks against each other's as we bear-hugged on the dance floor; finally retiring to banquettes where we'd pantomime deep conversations about love and loyalty, never managing to escape the swamp of faux profundity that alcohol traps you in—no longer provided a reliable reset from what bored us. Most transplants I knew had moved to New York because of the quick and diverse ways to achieve ecstasy (a once-in-a-lifetime show, landing a hard-won assignment, actual ecstasy), at the expense of basically everything else in our lives. After more than ten years of tapping at the lever, many of my friends seemed to reach an existential crossroads. Some sought out harder and more acute thrills. Others chased the highs through work, through bigger paychecks, more demanding projects. The wedding snowball began to pick up—one year, I had not been to a single wedding; the next year, I had four. After eight years of dating, my boyfriend, Nathan, and I came to realize that we were in it together—that among the many blessings of our relationship was the mutual conviction that the other—and us as an *us*—expanded our capacities to go, as individuals, to places that would otherwise be too difficult, too risky, too expensive, too lonely. Nathan and I exchanged vows in his mother's backyard, and in front of our friends and families, he promised that he had loved every version of me and told me he'd love every version to come. I promised him the same.

Our thirties had arrived.

We left New York without much ceremony—a small goodbye at a bar, an evening spent patching up holes in the drywall with a yogurt-sized tub of spackle, a night on a blow-up air mattress after the movers lassoed all our belongings together with packer's tape and tucked them inside a truck—and flew to Minnesota with eleven suitcases. There, we loaded up the car Qing no longer drove, an eleven-year-old SUV that she mostly used to make the five-minute commute to the office, driven so infrequently it still had its new car smell, to make our way west. The whole business of moving to Los Angeles reeked of cliché. Every step in the process, no matter if psychological or clerical, was one I knew was coming and anticipated because I had read about it in essays from people who had done it decades and generations before me. My life in 2019 felt like I was watching a movie I had seen before and did not like very much, but the remote was in another room. It was easier to just doze off.

For many related reasons, this was also the year that I began to enjoy weed. I had hated it in college when I tried it for the first time, sucking through a glass bong as someone else lowered a lighter to the packed bowl. Everyone at Berkeley smoked weed with fluid, practiced motions, which looked as sophisticated as Jean Seberg lighting a cigarette. I was always self-conscious of revealing that I had no idea what I was doing, so I'd inhale as quickly as I could when someone would tell me to pull, intent on doing a good and complete job, and then realize within seconds that I'd made a mistake: My lungs would turn into a scorched balloon, exactly the feeling of a bad urinary tract infection, which would radiate outward, pure panic sizzling every nerve ending. I'd cover my mouth to will myself not to cough, and giant gusts of white smoke would erupt through my fingers like I was a cartoon steam train, as some folks would chuckle in the knowing but nonjudgmental way of people who smoked weed regularly. "You all right? That was a big rip," someone would say as I slid, mute and panicked, into the same internal place I used to visit as a kid when Qing would get mad. Though the feeling would only last a minute or so, it was always so terrifying that I could never really enjoy the high that followed.

But in New York, the weed was, according to my California friends, weak and terrible, which meant it was perfect for me. The dealers, too, also began to carry weed in other forms that I much preferred: I enjoyed my cannabis from a pretty disposable pen that lit up like a robot tampon, and ate it as tiny cubes from a circular tin, tasting like what I thought Turkish delights ought to.

What I liked most about weed was how it allowed me to turn into a paperweight, growing heavy and substantial yet totally inconsequential. There were no hangovers and the only toll I'd pay was having to pass through the panicky part, which never really subsided but did get easier to reckon with once I knew the terrain: the quick inflammation in the beginning, the sustained shrillness during its peak, and then the abrupt ending, relief coming through like a puncture, the imprinted well of where the panic had carved out of me quickly flooded with muted pleasure. And the sleep that came afterward was divine.

I did not realize I missed being still until I realized I loved smoking weed. At that point, I was constantly on the move, both geographically and mentally. I had been traveling nonstop, and nearly all of it was for work. I had covered Fashion Weeks for nearly a decade and realized at one point that I had been to Milan more often than I had been to Staten Island. *Style Out There* sent me on a series of back-to-back flights that bounced me around from country to country. But what was really exhausting was the mental work. Like so many digital newsrooms in the years after Trump was elected in 2016, my job had shifted gears. It had always been true that writing about fashion was also a struggle for legitimacy. It has always been that way for anyone writing about fashion, because there will always be people who love to point out that there are things more important than what we wear—which is technically true, but spiritually uninteresting. But after Trump's election, there was a significant cultural shift in which it became imperative to proclaim that the ways in which we seek pleasure are justifiable beyond the simple truth that pleasure seems to be crucial to a life worth living.

The beginning steps were awkward and mostly embarrassing—I tried to find connections between fashion and the world writ large through any means, no matter how tenuous and speculative, oftentimes drawing upon the most painful-sounding parts of my personal experience in order to achieve connection. But my most-read work, the articles and videos that resonated most with people, centered on how subcultural fashion trends were a vehicle to discuss why those who dressed in an outsider way were outsiders in the first place.

There was so much that was deemed important that it was easy to feel unimportant, and, over time, it became clear that so many readers were suffering the same flavor of pain, yelling in various ways that they were unsupported, unaffirmed, unseen. And so I wrote the same fashion article in infinite forms, and the subtext became a refrain, a journalistic mission of sorts: We see you. You are seen.

But at home, on my couch, I looked forward to my nightly disappearing act. Whenever that come-up feeling of panic would dissipate, and relief would surge through my body like a beautiful disease, I would sometimes think about Qing's hands. They were perpetual fists, her thumbs tucked into the fingers. Even while her right hand maneuvered a fork or a pair of chopsticks, her left would stay balled up. Without a single way to force her body to soften, to snip the ropes of obligation she strained to keep taut, those fists just stayed that way. Qing literally had no way to loosen up.

But then the weed would do its job, and the rope connected to this thought would sever, sending Qing's fists tumbling far away.

●

A YEAR after our trip to Versailles, Qing started planning another trip to Europe. This time, she and Dexin would go to Amsterdam along with a pair of friends of theirs they liked to hike with on the weekends. I was proud of her newfound confidence, though I found the circumstances odd. For one, her friends had talked about voting for Trump, an unimaginable decision for both Qing and my father, who had only voted for Democratic presidential candidates since the year they became citizens. They were stunned that someone so obviously corrupt and ill-equipped could be a serious candidate, never mind the country's president, but more so than that, Qing could not believe what he had unlocked in people—Trump's bombastic rhetoric changed people that Qing had thought she knew. There had always been people who were snobbish, mean-spirited, and self-righteous, but they had had the good sense to save it for hushed conversations. Now, they seemed to be proud of these qualities and saw them as evidence of their superiority. With a sinking feeling, Qing listened as some of her friends said that their tax dollars were subsidizing lazy new immigrants. They left China because they were stifled by socialism, they said. They did not come to America to lose all their hard-earned money to people who didn't want to work for themselves.

"Really? You come to this country for education, not to be rich," Qing would mutter to me over the phone, saying what she hadn't dared the evening before. "If you had běnshì, you would not be use Head Start and food stamps at all. You would not take scholarship. And you think Trump will like someone like you, when you speaking English this bad?"

But these were their friends. They had survived in this country alongside one another. For that alone, Qing respected them, even if she could not understand the correlation between the pride they had and the hate they now harbored. And so she asked them to simply stop talking about politics. She had been consistent about what she thought her entire life: that no one is more entitled to a safe and loving life than anyone else is. Her opinion was her own, though she'd give it to them if they asked. But if they wanted to debate her so they could prove her wrong, to belittle her for her beliefs, that would mean they didn't respect her. Without respect, that'd be the end.

Qing lost a few friends between 2016 and 2020. She cut off some who deliberately ignored her boundaries, and she watched her WeChat groups dwindle. The sad truth of it was that friends she could actually speak to, in her own language, in person, were a precious, rare thing. Each loss was its own devastation. Then again, were they really speaking the same language anymore?

But the friends she was planning on going to Amsterdam with really did respect her. They respected her boundaries, her opinions, her decisions, and her reactions. They respected that she didn't have a passion for hiking like they did, but that she did love art and music, and that she had a different understanding of what was "bad" and what was "good." Amsterdam was not their first choice, and neither was it Qing's. But they bent to one another. That meant something.

Political differences aside, the second issue that did not

come with a tidy answer, at least not right away, was why they'd be going to Amsterdam, a city that, up until that point, had never come up in conversation, as far as I could remember. My parents were not the urban biking type, and their tastes in cities veered more toward large and imposing rather than cute and charming; I was fairly sure that the more prurient reasons that compel first-timers to visit the legalize-it-all city didn't apply to Qing and Dexin. Picking Amsterdam seemed like an accident. Until, that is, I was pulling into a parking spot along one of the hairpin residential streets of the Airbnb we had been renting in Los Angeles, and I received a text from Qing: "Do u recommend me to try weeds?"

I'm unaware of the Chinese word for marijuana. I'm sure it exists, but for my parents' generation, and the rest of us first-gen kids, there was just one word for drugs: dú, which is the same word for *poison*. You could xī dú, chī dú, yòng dú—*suck poison*, *eat poison*, and *use poison*—which is somewhat helpful as context clues to which drug anyone was talking about, but I suspected, and still do, that the only thing most Chinese parents know about drugs is that bad people do them. Once, Qing relayed a story to me about a friend of hers who found a dime bag in her daughter's room. "Marijuana!" she whispered. "A small bag of white powder!" I did not correct her.

The car idled as I struggled to type out a response. I had

been in Los Angeles for a month and a half now, feeling very much bruised and sore from having to relearn years of muscle memory to accomplish every little task—everything from commuting to work to engaging in small talk. I offended people with my Brooklyn-honed driving, which was slow yet aggressive. I offended people by asking them what they did for work, for offering a contrarian opinion about a movie they had just seen, for setting up drinks across town on a weekday. I walked to get groceries like I had always done, and—shocked by the assortment of handsome produce that I couldn't leave on the shelves—pulled my neck attempting to haul everything home, and couldn't look to the right for weeks. I got sunburned almost immediately, and long-dormant seasonal allergies kicked my ass. I couldn't figure out how to stay hydrated. I had to relearn how to talk, to walk, to dress, to drive. Eventually, I knew I'd have to relearn how to earn money, to be in a family, to make friends.

The scattered restlessness I felt in New York now had places to go. I was exhausted, but I felt more energized than I had been in a long time.

It helped that I felt I could do it for no reason other than I had done it many times before. I felt like I was two again, eighteen again, like I was twenty-two again. It was uncharted territory, and it felt familiar, dear.

But back to the text—this was new territory, too. I asked

Qing how much she already knew about weed. "Some. You put in nose," she said in response.

I tried to make it as easy as possible, texting her information about a coffee shop in Amsterdam that was run by a mother and daughter who catered to first-timers. Qing asked if she should start practicing by smoking cigarettes, and I realized how serious this was for her, and so I gave her a script and a plan to use: She'd tell the workers at the counter that she had never had cannabis before, and she thought she might like an indica edible, something soft and relaxing. If they agreed, she'd eat just half of a dose in the coffeehouse garden while my dad was with her. After an hour, she'd gauge whether she wanted to take the other half. There was a bike path nearby so she could people-watch if she wasn't in the mood to talk. If she wasn't feeling well, the coffeehouse was a short trip back to their hotel.

I did not tell her about the parts during which she might panic, not wanting to scare her. But I was scared for her. I hoped she was not also predisposed to that feeling, or that she'd accidentally get too high, feeling judged and alone. Worse yet, I feared it wouldn't work at all.

A FEW WEEKS LATER I was celebrating my birthday in my new home (Qing was happy to hear there were no shared walls, and thus no threat of snakes), with a handful of my best friends. My friend Isha made dinner for everyone in the kitchen, which was big enough that we could all comfortably fit inside, some people idling with wine and others chopping or stirring. It felt so extravagant to not have to negotiate our bodies because of a lack of space, to not have to forever be clearing off the counter space, to not have to throw open a window because of the accumulated steam from the pots and our breath.

We did not yet have a couch or bookshelves, and the curtains had just been hung that afternoon. But we did have a big dining table that we had moved—for the purposes of the party—to the center of the biggest room at the front of the house, like I was some Gilded Age scion hosting dinner in a ballroom. It was the kind of evening that would have been impossible for me to have had in New York, and I was warm from orange wine and a feeling of bounty.

The home itself was a quarter of the size of the Eden Prairie house, and yet it was the biggest place I had lived in since I left for college. It had been built just shy of a hundred years ago by developers in the twenties, and we had bought it with the intention of living in it for the rest of our lives. Our forever home, I told Nathan. The idea of not having to move unless I chose to move filled me with relief.

My phone buzzed. I glanced down at it as the conversation roiled around me. It was Qing:

> Hi Connie, we went to La Tertulia Coffeeshop yesterday and I told the daughter of the store owner about me- first time, never smoke before, my daughter recommended this store . . . , and she explained a lot to and gave me the weeds that first time people should try, but I said yes I will try this at hotel (you told me) and really want to try smoking style, she said I don't know how to inhale . . . not recommend me trying . . . I ate 1/3 of weed (tasted like sesame and little chocolate mixed feeling, like yummy cookie) at 12am, about 15 minutes later I felt sleepy but no other feeling so I went to bed 12:30am and slept until 6:30am this morning then back to sleep . . . the alarm woke me up at 7am, i never have this kind experience (back to sleep and 6 more than 6 hours sleep)? around 40 years since 1980 my college time, all kinds of sleeping pills didn't work for me. I like this weed that makes sleeping well. Thanks Connie I love this!

I knew that the text must have taken her nearly an hour to compose, typed out with one finger, her eyes peering above the tops of her reading glasses. A photo of the lollipop arrived soon after the text, her fingers holding the stem like it was a prize tulip, the white hotel sheets and beige-painted walls of the generic hotel room fuzzy in the background.

She had done drugs. She had *slept*.

"What are you smiling at?" my friend Nancy asked me. I relayed the news, and everyone whooped. Most of my friends were first-generation immigrants themselves. "Isn't she almost sixty?" someone asked. "She must be the first Asian mom to get into weed, but then again, Qing's always been a trendsetter."

When I spoke with Qing over the phone after her trip was over, she told me how Amsterdam had opened up to her that evening. There were so many museums, and everyone rode bikes, and sex was advertised on the street. There were tall white people who were friendlier than anyone she had ever met; one day, they had all boarded a bus going in the wrong direction, and once they realized what they had done, they scrambled to pull out a map to figure out where they had gone wrong and how to get back on track. Another passenger observed the commotion and patiently helped them navigate their way back so they wouldn't have to risk getting lost again. This happened over and over, and Qing noted that the people who had helped them were always dressed beautifully (her highest praise), in unassuming wool coats and well-cared-for scarves. Van Gogh, Qing was surprised to find out, painted those sunflowers exactly like he saw them, living creatures who existed with him on the verge of sanity: part nightmare, part daydream. The Van Gogh exhibit frightened her in its strangeness and familiarity. I asked whether Dexin enjoyed the exhibit. He didn't get it, she told me, her voice notably compassionate instead of braggy. She, on the other hand, couldn't stop thinking about it.

And then there was the whole "socialist" business that she was sent headlines about on WeChat. She knew that the world was full of socialist countries, many of which echoed the socialist principles that were evident in even the Chinese nursery rhymes she knew by heart. This Dutch socialism did not feel like her socialism. The one she knew was supposed to engender feelings of kinship, peace, and contentedness, but she saw how it had also led so many people to solipsism, jingoism, isolation. But in Amsterdam, fresh and rested, she wondered if there could be a reason for the lack of tension she felt from the people she encountered there. What made people more generous, more patient, more relaxed? Was it their relationship to money? Was it how they lived and worked? Was it the weed? The trust they had in one another to join or disassociate, to indulge or be responsible, without oversight and shame?

This weed lollipop was a rototiller, razing what had

hardened during her decades in America. She could find new paths, ideas, and politics. She could explore as she pleased. At fifty-eight years old, Qing stumbled across an awakening. All it took for it to happen was for her to finally fall asleep.

# EIGHT

# Homecomers
## *China Part II*

A fter Amsterdam, Qing became obsessed with understanding why Amsterdam was so *nice*. She was especially fascinated by its socialism and found herself wanting to know more. Julia offered to accompany Qing before she would begin a medical residency in the fall. And so it came to be that my mother made plans to visit three Scandinavian countries in the spring of 2020—Sweden, Denmark, and Norway.

Qing had been planning to use all of her accrued vacation days from her job, reserving some days in February to return to China to see my paternal grandparents, who had been bedbound for the past few years. Julia and I decided we'd tag along, because it had been nearly a decade since the three of us had traveled to China together, and we had never been during the Lunar New Year. We decided to tack on a few more places, too—Taiwan and South Korea for the three of us before heading to China, Japan for just the two of them afterward. This year, 2020, would be Qing's world tour.

I bought the leap-frog plane tickets while a second pregnancy test marinated in the sink.

The first stick was positive, but I wanted to be sure, even though I already felt certain. I had been pregnant once before, just the month prior, and spent a day collecting positive pregnancy tests while my body urgently broadcast that we were in uncharted territory, nausea sitting at the bottom of my throat. My brain felt like a foam cushion, which wasn't an unpleasant feeling, exactly, but it made thinking any thoughts an involved, arduous task. Trying to suss out something simple (where I put my socks, whether I was cold) was like a desultory, wine-drunk conversation with myself. My jaw was sore and painful, the hinges clicking with every chew. The very next day, I woke up with a heavy period, and my doctor confirmed I had had a chemical miscarriage. He patted me on the back and sounded as if he were congratulating me, though it didn't seem like something to celebrate—"It's all very normal, and I'll see you again soon"—and I left his office feeling relieved and just a little sad. Afterward, Nathan took me to Malibu to walk along the empty shore, and I pocketed a smooth rock to remind myself how it felt on this day to have taken a step in so foreign a direction.

One month later, I woke up with the exact same physical discomfort. Two lines revealed themselves on one test. Then another. I waited for my period, and it didn't come. And so I just waited.

I was cognizant enough of the risk of miscarriage that I followed the conventional wisdom to keep it to myself until the second trimester, but I was not bothered by the anxiety of keeping it to myself; I was too distracted by the hormones. Though I looked exactly the same, my insides were in turmoil. The physicality of pregnancy felt awfully similar to dread. I could not sleep at night, I could not sleep in, I could not feel hungry, and I could not feel satisfied. I could not feel at ease.

I had always knocked back this sensation by taking action. If I was worried about work, I'd put in more hours to get ahead of my tasks. If I was nervous about an appointment, I'd schedule my day to the brim to distract myself. But this was different from anything else I had ever planned for. My entire life had been, in part, about preparing for the future, though most of these plans—moving away from home, landing a job, finding a life partner—still came with an escape hatch. But becoming pregnant, if things went well, did not. I couldn't go backward, quit motherhood, go home, abandon ship. In nine months' time, my life *would be* completely different, and I had no idea what to expect between now and then, much less from then onward.

All I knew was that those hormones—the ones that were supposed to turn you into an animal who'd gnaw off their own arm to protect their unborn child—were no fun. Moreover, I couldn't stop calling the baby an "it," even when we found out the gender, even when we decided on a name. The lack of affection I felt worried me, and I turned my attention to other ways to prove my love—or show it, I suppose—by setting up a spreadsheet of things I needed to acquire for the nursery, downloading pregnancy apps, and modifying my diet.

My diet. I am generally an enthusiastic and greedy eater. I love everything about eating: preparing food, consuming it, indulging in it, being transported by it. And though my relationship with food has thankfully never been disordered, it has always been abnormal. The ideas I have about nourishment are a reaction to Qing, who is not an emotional eater, does not particularly like the act of eating itself, and treats food like medicine—a tool to administer nutrition and cures. Some of the principles of her very specific food ideology stem from a history of lack (if my sister or I didn't want to finish our meals, we at least had to finish the high-value proteins); some were cultural (those awful sea cucumbers); but most were personal. Stomachaches could be cured with a fruit snack. Packaged foods were the products of science, and thus better for you than raw foods. A McDonald's Filet-O-Fish or Arby's Beef 'n Cheddar sandwich were hǎo dōngxī, *good stuff*. Growing up, I regularly showed up at the bus stop in the morning with a Drumstick ice cream cone fetched from the freezer; according to Qing, it was a perfect breakfast food since it contained protein (nuts), carbs (the cone), dairy (the ice cream), and, best of all, I wouldn't have anything to throw away afterward. It was certainly no more sugary than the breakfast cereals the other kids at the bus stop had eaten that morning. Recently she read a chumbox article that used dubious logic to claim that coffee was "healthy," and so she now drinks a cup each morning, black, like a tonic.

But it would be a mistake to assume these tactics are insincere or a quirky thing a quirky person would like to believe. Qing's attempts at healthfulness are genuine, and started before she could remember. She likes to say that she cannot help any of it: Because of her personality, she *made* herself physically fragile with a weak constitution, and it was her own fault that she could not sleep and her hair was thin, that it took her twice the amount of food to absorb half the amount of nutrients. When she was eight, Qing had been asked by some well-meaning ayi whether she'd rather be eternally beautiful, smart, or healthy. After days of deliberation, she grudgingly picked smart, though she would have preferred to be beautiful, an answer she felt confident about until decades later. After I had left for college, the daily stomachaches Qing had endured suddenly became much, much worse. In the emergency room, she learned she had an extreme case of ulcerative colitis, her lower intestines a long tract of blisters. Critically depleted of nutrition and in a high degree of pain, she was monitored in the hospital for weeks on a high-dose course of steroids. Before she began to get better, Qing hedged her bets and prayed to all the gods she could name that she had changed her mind: She'd rather be healthy than smart, and certainly more than beautiful. If she was healed, she'd never take her health for granted again.

When she left the hospital, she was just eighty pounds, her already birdlike frame reduced to hollow bones and vellum skin. Her body looked like an upside-down fork missing its center tines, and she carried herself in the inwardly warped, fearfully defensive way that chronically thin women do, like they are too frail to withstand the gravity of their souls, which seem denser than other people's. She had always been thin, and it was something that she had accepted—and felt both lucky and exasperated to have found herself in eras and places where she had been ashamed of such a thing, and then was supposed to be proud of it, and she would respond to people all the time who asked her what her secret was, how was she able to maintain her figure, how was she *just so tiny*: that she was this way in spite of her best efforts.

After her hospitalization, Qing finally began putting on weight again through a carefully observed diet that was part medically prescribed and part discovered via trial and error. Fibrous foods like raw vegetables were to be avoided (more evidence that they were unhealthy for the larger population), as were big meals and spicy things. On her own, Qing found that eating two ziplock bags full of lean short ribs and eight eggs a day kept her colitis at bay. Fruit snacks didn't aggravate it; neither did Costco-sized tubs of cashews and peanuts. She ate constantly, and her kitchen island turned into a grazing buffet, covered in medium-sized bowls of dried and fresh fruit, fancy nuts, Haw Flakes wrapped like a stack of quarters, and peanut butter cups. More than cold-pressed juice or a lush grain bowl, this tableau of snacks, to Qing, was the picture of health.

When Qing was pregnant with me, she followed a strict diet that left such a negative impression on her that it was the only thing she ever mentioned about being pregnant, and she mentioned it incessantly: It was a daily diet of hard-boiled eggs, large quantities of lean pork and tilapia, under-seasoned green-leafed vegetables, and hideous amounts of walnuts. The amount of each food would change as the fetus-me grew, but it was pretty much the same mix for nine months. It sounded pretty good to me, but she spoke about it without fondness or nostalgia. "Suffering," she'd always say, dramatically shuddering like a tree being uprooted. "Every day suffering."

Finally, I knew what she was talking about. For the first time in my life, my body fought back against food. Eating was no longer enjoyable. I shed weight as I grew a person, only able to handle ready-to-eat foods that were somewhat tangy but mostly bland: store-bought potato salad, cheap sourdough bread, Haribo candy spaghetti. Putting anything in my mouth that I did not want—any meat whatsoever, or walnuts that left behind a cottonmouth film on my tongue, or *that many* whole eggs—was inconceivable. I wondered how many nutrients I was actually ingesting with my drugstore cold-case diet, but I could not dredge up the willpower to try harder. It was selfish of me. It was juvenile. But I was already ceding so much of my body to a phantom I could not communicate with, and there was still so much time left before I'd get it back.

QING WORRIED whether these long flights would affect the fetus, but it was fine: I slept the whole time. I've never had trouble sleeping on flights. They were, and still are, black holes of consciousness to me. By the time the engines turn on, I am usually half-asleep already, my face tucked into the space between the plane window and my neck pillow, my ankles crossed and tucked into the far corner of my foot space, my hands tucked under my thighs to keep me in place. If I have the chance to spread out, even better. If I'm already tired, there's no waking me up. Once, after a week-long trip to Tokyo, I flew back to New York with my editor, who marveled, once we landed, that I was out for the entire thirteen-hour flight. *Did you not have to pee? Weren't you hungry?* I don't know, I told her. I might have been, but I couldn't be sure. I was asleep.

(An aside about sleeping on flights: There is no trick to it. Either you can sleep or you cannot sleep. Foam neck pillows can help good sleepers sleep faster, as do eye masks and noise-canceling headphones. Pills work, too. But if you cannot sleep on flights, the "sleep" you'll experience will make the time pass quicker, but it won't provide any rest— or so I've heard. Those sleep gadgets that used to be advertised in *SkyMall*—the ones that strap on to your own headrest and cradle your face and upper chest like a jock-strap; the oversized foam wedges meant to be placed on your tray table and laid on against like a sleepy storybook bear against a log—turn one's struggle into a pitiable spectator event. Do not waste your money!)

Taiwan was our first stop, and once we arrived and it was clear that the flight had been soothing for me (and thus, I assumed, the fetus), Qing's concerns were quickly replaced by another worry. Her sister, Li Bai, had sent us a message on WeChat: A highly contagious flu was going around, and we might want to bring extra face masks if we had them handy. A CNN article popped up in my notifications that the epicenter of this coronavirus seemed to be in Wuhan, and we were glad that it was five-hundred-some miles away from where we'd be in China. Nevertheless, Julia doled out the masks she had brought with her: simple baby-blue rectangles in a thick stack, and a few duck-billed super masks that were called N95s that she promised she'd show us how to wear if things got really bad. "But then that'd mean we were in some kind of horror-movie pandemic," she joked.

Qing found Taiwan charming; she loved reading the street names out loud, which were cutesified compared to the ceremonious names of the roads in mainland China. My sister and I tried to eat everything, waking up at 4:30 a.m. to stand in line to get dòujiāng and yóutiáo—*soybean milk and savory doughnuts*—and would bounce from twenty-four-hour hot pot restaurants to beef noodle shops, labyrinth-like night markets to laboratory-like dessert chains, until my nausea would show up, leaving me dry heaving downwind from a stinky tofu stand.

Seoul was fascinating to Qing: how everything was so neat and tidy and nearly identical, including the clothes and makeup people wore. People were wrapped in varying shades of gray and brown, with dewy makeup that made sharpened nose bridges look as slick as ice luges, eyes made up to look perpetually wide and puppy-dog sad.

By then, the phone notifications were coming in more frequently—now, from *The New York Times* and the *Los Angeles Times*—but my aunt continued to reassure us that it would not get to Jinan, that there were no cases at all in Shandong province. The day before we were supposed to fly from South Korea to China, Qing sat on the hotel bed for hours, scrolling through her phone, reading everything. Julia asked, "Where do you want to go to eat dinner?" I asked, "Should we take a detour to see this neighborhood?" She didn't respond to any of our questions. Instead, she grew more and more silent, and more and more mad. "What's wrong?" we'd entreat, and the lines between her eyebrows would sharpen. "You girls go," she'd say, almost accusingly. "Mom too scared."

She was in a fugue state, unable to talk or move. She would just sit and seethe, and demand to be left alone. We'd push and she'd dig in her feet, and I got angry seeing her like this, so fixated on the wrong thing, so convinced of disaster. My sister and I knew how much gravity Qing's mood had on the rest of us. No matter how happy we were, if Qing was dour, we would all eventually join her (at the same time, if we were in a glum mood and Qing was hyperactive, we'd liven up, too). But tonight, I was even more stubborn. I was in no mood to be in a bad mood, especially on a vacation that felt like it was the last of something.

Julia and I were too cavalier about COVID-19. Of course we were. We had been in China during the SARS outbreak in the early 2000s; I had gotten H1N1 the third month I moved to New York. Headlines about travelers spreading deadly viruses like Ebola were sensational and fearmongering. It was xenophobic, too, we told Qing; if this particular flu had come from anywhere else but China, it would not be made out to be this awful thing. We'll be careful, like we always were, and wear our masks. The fact that we even brought masks meant we were being overly cautious. And besides, if there was any government in the world who'd know how to deal with a highly transmissible flu, it'd be the East Asian countries we were already in, which had already dealt with outbreaks and had made mask-wearing a critical part of their public hygiene. That last part seemed to relax Qing: Americans would never wear masks, Qing concluded. We were safer here than anywhere else. She'd come to dinner.

The walk to Hongdae from our hotel was long but lively; it was a frigid Saturday night, and it seemed like every young person in Seoul was out that evening. The sun had set long ago but you could hardly tell, the glow from millions of LED lights made the streets feel like a movie set. We linked arms as we walked, and took turns navigating

the winding path with an unreliable Google Maps app, taking wrong turns, getting annoyed with one another, and
playing a dangerous game of chicken by choosing to push
one another's buttons and backing off at the last moment.
By the time we reached the barbecue spot, we were spent
and glad that there was a wait before there'd be an empty
table so we had an excuse to sit in silence. The three of us
kept warm inside a waiting area that was enclosed by plastic tarps, our collective breath leaving a film of beady condensation.

The food was wonderful, even though meat and I were
still not on speaking terms. I actually ate enough to feel
full, the first time that had happened since I had become
pregnant. Afterward, we crossed the street to a boutique
department store, where I picked out a brown shearling
coat intercut with banana-yellow nylon, and Qing bought
an armful of fun dresses that fit her perfectly. The mood
was restored, and we walked back to the hotel with more
patience in the tank for inaccurate navigation. Still, Qing
was quieter than usual. Back in our rooms and having finished packing for our early morning departure, she stayed
up all night reading articles about COVID on WeChat. She
tried to reassure herself. Julia and Connie were not worried. They knew what they were doing. Julia was going to
be a doctor, and she understood medicine. Connie spoke
so confidently about which articles were fake news and

which were not. She seemed to think things would be okay. Julia did, too. It will be fine, she told herself.

❦

WE FLEW TO CHINA the next morning, and arrived in Jinan in high spirits. The airport was busy with the preholiday rush, and we ran through our agenda in the car as we drove to my aunt's apartment. On that first night, we ate at a restaurant to celebrate Laoye's ninetieth birthday. There, I told him that I was expecting, and he told me it'd be a girl. *You can't know that*, I responded. My laolao, seated next to me, smacked her lips in faux frustration and jabbed her elbow against my arm: "*He thinks he knows everything*," she said, glowering, in Mandarin. He sat up straight as an arrow and joined in. "*Nonsense. I* know." It had been at least three generations since there had been a boy born in the family, he explained. It was not possible to have our blood and conceive a boy. But at my behest, among the handful of girl names he had been saving for us, he wrote down a name in Chinese that'd fit a boy, in case the pattern was broken. Yunfei. *To fly among the clouds.*

Later that evening, Qing told me there was more to it. *To fly among the clouds*, she repeated. *And be worthy of it.*

The next morning, literally overnight, the entire country was locked down.

The speed at which it happened was incredible. Only one person per household was allowed to grocery shop, and so my aunt went by herself, not knowing how many meals she'd have to spin them into (she was optimistic: just a few days, no doubt). Slapdash public service announcements began showing up on TV in between the commercial breaks of my cousin's daughter Jiajia's favorite show, *Dà Tóu Érzi, Xiǎo Tóu Bābā—Big Head Son, Little Head Papa*—a bizarre but compelling children's program we watched every afternoon. Later, back in America, I would think of this cartoon at my first major ultrasound appointment, as the technician told me that the baby had both a very large head and penis, and it took a long series of back-and-forths until I was assured that neither was a medical issue. On the ultrasound screen that was projected ahead of me, the baby was a cluster of circles, like a crude sketch of a teddy bear. In the printouts I took home afterward, I searched for evidence of my big-head self or my little-head husband, and thought about Big Head Son's mom, a character with an average-sized skull whom they merely called Apron Mama.

"Be good and obedient, and have a quiet New Year's! This will help us all be safe. This is your biggest contribution to fighting the epidemic," the public service commercials for children cheerfully exclaimed. Jiajia, who had just turned four, thought it was all so much fun, all these āyís there to play with her all day, every day. She spoke with the vocabulary and diction of a child who had grown up around only adults, a sign of meaningful privilege and wealth, having never *had to* go to daycare or preschool, never *had to* be one among many, since she was so many people's first priority. She was the first and only great-grandchild, and received those universally recognized perks of being so. She was quick to tantrums because everyone else was quick to placate. She didn't so much walk around as she announced herself with her steps. How she automatically opened her mouth as she was fed every bite of every meal she ever ate, not making eye contact with the food deliverer until she remembered a story, a song, a question. Her confidence that she always was right, wanted, and belonged. To me, it felt familiar, but not personally so. It was how I always imagined American childhoods were like.

The circumstances of Jiajia's birth are not mine to tell, but Jiajia was the best thing to come out of a brief marriage that had already fallen apart by the time she was conceived. As such, her grandparents—my aunt, Li Bai, and her husband— were Jiajia's primary caregivers while my cousin worked. And even though China's one-child policy was over, Jiajia would likely remain an only child—my cousin joked that she had had a taste of partnered life and decided that it was easier to do things alone.

But, of course, my cousin wasn't alone. She was a part of our family—a family that has always been a tribe of mostly women, anticipating one another's needs, worrying about one another's futures, easing one another's discomforts. Much of this was invisibly orchestrated by my aunt, Li Bai, who was now retired, but seemed to be working harder than ever. There were lots of people who relied on Li Bai. My laolao and laoye, who were finding it more difficult to get around by themselves, but were more proud and stubborn than they were enfeebled, which meant Li Bai had to resort to sneaking around in order to help out. Her daughter, who was going through a terrible divorce to a terrible man, whose terrible family would not quit coming up with new convoluted ways to make things worse. Jiajia, whose temper was fiercer than any of theirs.

On the news, reporters talked about how multigenerational living arrangements, the norm throughout China, was the number-one cause of spread. The best thing you could do, they said, was nothing. The commercials said the same: *The holidays are about family. Show them you love them by staying home and wearing a mask outside.* I thought about life in America, our orphan family of four, and how not living at home—or even being close to it—had always been the goal. Geographical, professional, and financial independence was something like a family value, so clearly imprinted on myself and Julia by Qing. Here in Jinan, I thought about how intertwined things were, and that though my family operated like a matriarchy, the trajectories of our lives still veered wildly off course because of the whims of our men. The direction these thoughts were headed in made me nervous, and so I turned my attention to Jiajia, who had her hands clasped behind her back, reciting a nursery rhyme so common even I knew it:

Xiǎo yànzi, chuān huāyī,
Nián nián chūntiān lái zhèlǐ,
Wǒ wèn yànzi nǐ wèi shá lái,
Yànzi shuō zhèlǐ de chūntiān zuì měilì.

Little swallow, dressed in color
Every spring comes to visit
I asked the sparrow, why do you come?
The sparrow said the spring days here are the most beautiful.

I started to clap, but she wasn't done. The second stanza was unfamiliar.

Xiǎo yànzi, gàosu nǐ
Jīnnián zhèlǐ gèng měilì
Wǒmen gài qǐle dà gōngchǎng
Zhuāng shàngle xīn jīqì
Huānyíng nǐ chángqī zhù zài zhèlǐ.

Little sparrow, let me tell you
It's even more beautiful this year
We built a large factory
Installed new machinery
We welcome you to live here forever.

"Good recitation!" My aunt and cousin clapped for Jia-jia, who had started grinning before she finished. She knew the ditty was a crowd pleaser.

"Wait . . . what?" I swiveled to Julia, raising my eyebrows. "Factories? Do you know this ending?"

"*We don't usually sing the second part*," Qing explained in Mandarin. "*I didn't remember what it was about.*"

"Communism," I answered in English.

Qing reached across the lacquered table for more wrapped diǎnxīn and picked up a sesame brittle. "No," she said mischievously, in English. "It's about travel. And trying to convince xiǎo yànzi to stop travel. But why would she?"

●

WITCHING HOUR starts at 7:00 p.m. and lasts for two straight hours. Every evening Jiajia will be hysterical, and depending on the caretaker whose nerves were the least frayed that day, either my cousin, my aunt, or my uncle will hold Jiajia's hand, wipe her tears, and lie next to her in bed until she falls asleep. The family had assumed the ritual would end as soon as Jiajia was old enough to reason. But when that time came, Jiajia out-reasoned them: "*Because I just WANT to cry*," Jiajia wails. "*I HAVE to cry.*"

They will try, of course, to explain that crying for so

long every night isn't good for Jiajia. It's not good for the adults, either, who have lots of things they should be doing. It's not good for their neighbors, who, upon seeing Jiajia in the courtyard, will ask whether her voice is hoarse. "It's not hoarse," Jiajia will respond, polite as ever. So why does she do it? The neighbors want to know. "*I WILL cry, I HAVE to.*"

It's Jiajia's responsibility to think about others, my relatives gently lecture her. She grins at them. "*It's my responsibility to CRY.*"

They laugh at this, but I know this is more a kindness to themselves than to Jiajia. Being a loving, responsible parent, according to my aunt, means hiding your laughter. While raising my cousin, she never allowed herself to make jokes or be silly. Each evening she would come home after work, and before walking in the front door, my aunt said that she'd take a moment to stiffen her upper lip before my cousin could see. Now that she's a grandmother, she's less strict, she supposes.

In China, women were not expected to perform the kind of emotional labor—paid or otherwise—we recognize in America. It wasn't until I had been visiting China on my own, mostly for work, that I began to understand that it wasn't just a quirk of Qing's. Waiters never smiled, service workers never sugarcoated anything, wives and mothers didn't pretend to be upbeat when they were depressed. If anything, it was the reverse, to appear more droll, exasperated, humorless than you were—willing yourself not to smile so as not to spoil the baby, pretending you did not want to be near your grandma to keep her from getting sick. But there was still work to be done in order to make others more comfortable; it was just that in China this kind of extra labor was just plain-old *labor* labor: cutting up fruit into bite-sized pieces, waking up hours before dawn to run errands before the rest of the family woke up, taking the hour-long bus ride to hand-deliver lunch to the lao ren, our elderly relatives, so they could eat something home-cooked without having to risk lopping off the soft tips of their fingers again. After days spent slumped on Li Bai's couch, I thought about Qing's constant sternness when I was growing up. From this angle, it looked a little more like love.

The same few interviews with doctors at Wuhan hospitals were broadcast on the evening news; and the major compelling force during the televised Spring Festival Gala: "Staying at home is your greatest dedication and sacrifice against the epidemic," exclaimed host and news anchor Ouyang Xiadan. Dressed in a sequined tuxedo jacket and a red-satin bow-tie, his paternalistic speech took on a sideshow quality, made only more freaky as he introduced a troupe of acrobats who made human towers, three, four, five of them balanced on each other's thighs and pelvises, bending their bodies to accommodate the increasing burden.

Julia, Qing, and I laughed as we imagined the same thing

happening during the Oscars. Qing could laugh about it. That was good. Things were much worse than she had imagined during those days spent worrying in Seoul, though now that she was *in it*, the reality of the pandemic did not feel as oppressive as the fear of it. No one in her family was sick. There was no chance of them getting sick. Her family was too good at staying put, hunkering down, and surviving until spring.

Travel bans were implemented, another shocking development. "*Imagine them closing the borders in America*," said Qing in Mandarin.

"*Why wouldn't they?*" asked Li Bai.

"*They would never follow the laws.*" And then. "*We're too independent, too unused to sacrificing.*"

Li Bai chuckled, looking her younger sister in the eye. "*You all don't know what's good for you. Especially that one.*" She nodded at me.

Qing looked over, too, and then spoke honestly. "*It's true. Connie would never have survived in China. I would have been fine. But she would have been miserable.*" I was too nauseous to be offended, though the way Qing said it, with softness around the edges, made me think that she wanted me to know she was proud.

Plans to visit my dad's parents on the opposite end of the province were abandoned. The three of us would spend the remainder of our trip inside. A part of me was grateful.

I felt physically awful, nauseous, and tired as the baby who would probably not be named Yunfei continued to grow. An excuse to stay inside seemed like a gift. I remember thinking I could do this for a long, long time.

"Look," Qing remarked one evening, as she, Julia, and I were tucked in, width-wise, in the queen-sized bed in the spare room, the tops of our heads grazing the wall and our knees slightly bent so they didn't hang off the edge. Our faces were oriented toward the balcony where our laundry that Li Bai had done earlier that afternoon was air-drying, our socks and underwear hung next to Jiajia's little leggings, my uncle's undershirts, my cousin's pajamas. Through two sets of concrete walls, Jiajia's wails sounded almost like a dream. The three of us lay there, weary but not sleepy, warm and fed, regarding the wash that had been done by someone else.

# NINE

# Wŏde Mā Ya!
## *Los Angeles*

I never once considered the time we spent in quarantine in China to be the beginning of something. Even on the way to the airport—my uncle driving the three of us, often the only car on the road, through checkpoints manned by ghostly figures in papery hazmat suits, passing billboards advertising Lunar New Year festivities that never happened—it felt like the end of a hallucination. The death toll in Wuhan was astonishing, and the response seemed to break the laws of human capability: Hospitals were constructed in a few days' time; travel restrictions for the entire country were implemented with unreal efficiency. Sitting on the packed plane in a middle seat in my N95 mask that was pressed against every contour of my face just like Julia had instructed Qing and me to do, the condensation from my trapped breath pooling at my chin, I tried to lean into the delirium, to fast-forward to the other side of the journey where I could look back on all this in comfortable smugness. A bizarre thing that happened to *me* once.

A month later, Los Angeles began to shut down, too. As in China, it caught me off guard. One day, I was having dinner at a restaurant whose food and ambience left no lasting impression on me. The next, I was canceling my flight for a work trip I was supposed to take that afternoon. I stopped by Costco to pick up toilet paper and stock up on groceries, and the shelves were still full; the few people there were unharried. Coincidentally, Julia was in town. She had just come back from a cruise for a friend's bachelorette and was supposed to spend a week with me before leaving with Qing for their tour through Scandinavia. They'd end up canceling those flights, too, and Julia would live with us that summer, waiting out the time until she started her residency in the fall. She found a part-time job as a union organizer for veterans' hospital staff, and spent the late afternoons concocting elaborate dinners for the three of us at home (for that first quarantine weekend inside, she cooked a feast based on *Little House on the Prairie*, and she and I braided our hair into pigtails and ate apples 'n' onion and chicken pot pie). Nathan and I would work up until my due date, a rare pandemic goalpost, a treasured thing to have during a stretch of time that was absent of anything concrete. The banality of our everyday life—our silly routines, our little walks around the neighborhood with our recently adopted greyhound Hal, the simple festivities we planned for one another—was underscored by what we knew was happening outside the walls of our home: the death, the loss, the uncertainty.

My own paternal grandparents passed in quick succession, just weeks after we left China. The city was still so mangled from COVID that the cremation and funeral services were unattended. For weeks, Dexin existed by watching the screen of his WeChat for updates from his family, which came through sporadically, and were written to not cause further upset: "*Things are taken care of.*" These sparing updates, of course, had the opposite effect. *What is going on?* Dexin would want to respond. But he understood the subtext: *We love you. We made it. We don't need you here.* He wasn't going to make things harder for them.

I attempted to process all of this from the floor of my living room, where I was spending a lot of my days, trying to will the muscles along my spine to stop spasming, massaging the perimeter of my growing stomach that was hard as a rock and disconcertingly numb. But from inside the void, someone thrashed. I marveled at how something that I made and grew and harbored could also be so physically incomprehensible to me.

Of course, I tried to comprehend using all the tools I had in my reporter's kit: hear directly from primary sources, approach information with equal parts skepticism and curiosity, fill in your blind spots. I read hundreds of other people's birth plans about if they wanted drugs and, if so, exactly how much pain they wanted to experience before that; which music should be playing and when; when the baby should be held and by whom and for what purposes. It was a checklist of neurosis and hopes, ambitions and insecurities, the presence of self-awareness or the utter lack of it. I started reading them like they were dating profiles, searching for one that was me-shaped. I came across a handful that were from those with similar personalities—risk-averse and pro-intervention, disinterested in home comforts—or similar census designations—a healthy Chinese American in her mid-thirties—but reading myself in them did not fill me with a sense of affirmation or self-assurance. My obsessive desire to optimize was paralyzing. The notes app that was supposed to hold my birth plan never evolved past two items I had initially written as a joke: "Have baby. Don't die."

Qing arrived in Los Angeles two weeks before my due date, and we were as careful about it as people could be in those days before the vaccine. She mostly stayed in the spare bedroom we had not yet converted into a nursery, putting on her mask to go to the bathroom or fetch some food. After ten days, she emerged and we prepared together: I wrapped up my work duties, Nathan assembled the baby gear, Qing boiled chicken and steamed spinach to encourage milk production. Then we waited.

Marc Wang Yunfei Reese was born from an emergency C-section, a week after he was due to arrive, and after an induction and twenty-some hours of labor. The nurses who admitted me did not ask for a birth plan, which was the only thing that happened as I'd hoped. The doctor pulled Marc out of me covered in his own feces, limp and not breathing. But when he finally did, he writhed and gasped, then cried and blinked and clutched and twisted and smacked his lips like he was showing off all that he could do. They placed him on my neck and face for skin-to-skin contact, and I could not yet move my arms or open my eyes, but a clear thought sliced through the daze: His movements felt familiar to me, and this recognition brought me back to earth. After an evening in the nursery, the nurses told me that he did not sleep much, as newborns tend to do. "His eyes barely shut," they told me. "He was taking it all in!" Qing forwarded a video of Marc in his plastic bassinet to my laoye, who was in the hospital himself undergoing a series of tests; he had begun having trouble urinating, but shrugged it off as a minor ailment, nothing to be upset about, which marked the beginning of the last year of his life. *He looks just like Connie,* he relayed to my aunt, Li Bai, who noticed that Marc's toes—stacked on top of each other—looked exactly like my laoye's. But Marc's hands were Qing's hands. They were almost always balled up, even when he slept, but when we peeled back his fingers, we could see a curious set of palm lines: one fewer than what you were supposed to have, the deep-set creases curved away from one another without ever intersecting, back-to-back parentheses, punctuated by a deep ridge by the thumb—a short but deep life line, headed in the wrong direction, something that fortune-telling āyís would always point to on Qing's hand as curious, bizarre. "Look," Qing whispered on our first evening all together, Marc on her lap, his cracker-sized palm nestled in hers. "He's copying me."

Qing had allotted two weeks to spend with us after the birth, and we all realized the moment we left the hospital that it was not enough time. It took me an extraordinary amount of energy to move from the bed to the couch and back again, and I needed help wiping and bathing myself; my recovery itself was a two-person job, never mind the business of caring for a newborn. Those first weeks were a fever dream—an eternal stretch of the same order of business that went on in maddening loops every two hours— feed the baby, change the baby, hold the baby, try to get the baby to sleep, attempt a nap, google worries instead. I couldn't look at Qing when those two weeks were up, as she pulled her suitcase up the stairs with her one good arm, the other gingerly held against her torso, sore from cradling a newborn for hours on end. She gave me a hug goodbye without looking at me or Marc, who was asleep on my lap, and I knew it was because she too was crazed from worrying.

During those first few months, the apathy I felt toward my son in utero was replaced by an utter deluge of wonder and terror. It was not love. Not yet. But it was a state of responsibility so profound that it became corporeal: I could barely keep up with the places my body needed to go. Take breastfeeding, for instance, an act that I assumed was a mechanical process—two bags of milk with spigots for sapping—but turned out to be as close to an observed miracle as I've ever experienced, which is not to say that it was pleasant or amusing, because it was not. Rather, breastfeeding was a stupefying Rube Goldberg machine. From articles I googled during twilight, I learned that sucking began a physiological chain reaction that ultimately led to milk being released, the last step in a process that, for me, also included a profound collapse of the soul—a minor major depression—that always happened in the exact same way, a pattern-perfect pinch of the heart, a bottom falling away, and a spiritual flailing (lasting approximately thirty seconds). Breastfeeding felt like dread, but worse, because it was *supposed* to feel like euphoria. Bare-chested and with a warm thing clutched to me, I would sit there on the couch with my feet tucked in and my head bent over, breathing through the panic that spread from my breasts to my shoulders and down my limbs. By the time the panic reached my toes, milk would be trickling, and the sensation would dissipate.

I learned from lactation consultants that what I was experiencing was called the "let-down reflex," which struck me as hilarious. I also learned that most people experience letting down as a sensation of fullness and joy—but some people's bodies respond to the spike in prolactin and oxytocin with a corresponding crash in dopamine. There was not a vast amount of research on the subject, my doctor told me, but one study called it a "dysphoric milk-ejection reflex." I told him that I often tried to will myself not to let down when it was inconvenient—that sometimes, when I heard a baby crying on television, or my shirt grazed against my chest in a certain way, and I felt this sudden rise in doom and I was not supposed to be breastfeeding, I would will myself not to let down. *Just don't*, I'd reason with myself. I could will myself not to sneeze. I could will myself not to cry. Sometimes, on the living room floor, I could even will my back muscles to relax. I could will myself to jump, remain, flee, endure. Why couldn't I will myself to not leak milk? "You can't beat science," he laughed. *You can't do magic*, I heard.

The only thing *to* do was get used to it, or stop altogether. And so I attempted the former until the dozen daily episodes of gloom became routine. Five months in, a bad bout of thrush covered Marc's tongue in a film of white crud and left me raw and bleeding. That ended our breast-feeding experiment, and I found my way back to my own body—in control again, even from miracles.

THE YEAR I became a mother was also the first time in fifteen years that we had to skip our annual time-share vacation. Julia had, at this point, started her medical residency, which meant that she would be spending the holidays caring for COVID patients. Qing and Dexin would come to Los Angeles. For December, they'd quarantine in the basement guest room we had prepared for them, and join us for outdoor walks around the neighborhood. If nothing went awry and no one tested positive, we could then spend two weeks as a family before Dexin would have to return to Minnesota for work.

It had been three months since Qing had left, and Marc was no longer a newborn, but I had no sense of the time that had passed, or how things had improved or worsened, or changed at all. There was an election for which I had voted by mail, as had the majority of the home-bound country; Qing told me that her hiking friends, the Amsterdam couple, hadn't cast their votes for Trump, and I was so glad for so many reasons—of what it signaled about the country and people's abilities to change—but I was mostly glad for Qing. But besides that single day, I was stuck. The cyclical nature of caring for a baby dramatically limited my ability to sense what had changed. I knew that things had gotten technically easier as we learned little tricks and hacks to keep diapers on and soothe Marc when he was gassy. But things felt just as hard. The main issue was sleep: No one got enough of it, including Marc, who continued to fight against sleep, just as he did in the hospital nursery. If things went well, he would nap for forty-five minutes at a time, six or seven times a day—and sleep at night for a single three-hour stretch. But if things went poorly, he would nap in five-minute bursts, and sleep for just an hour.

Initially, I threw money at the problem, buying things off Amazon Prime at two in the morning that I hoped would be the magic bullet, like a plastic orange device with a speaker that played an Australian man's voice going "shhh" for thirty minutes at a time; a sleeping bag shaped like a gingerbread man because some babies (not mine) are soothed by the feeling of being straitjacketed with their arms up by their ears; a canister of magnesium after a family friend bleakly relayed how their baby never slept for longer than three hours at a time until the baby was nearly four years old and started taking magnesium supplements. I drank the bitter sleepy powder for days, hoping that some might make it into my breastmilk. After nothing worked, I turned to the process: How could I improve the way in which I got him to fall asleep? I tried walking him around the house, strapped to my chest, for a half hour before each nap. I'd bounce him in the middle of the day, tinfoil taped to the windows to block out every last ray of sunlight. But more often than not, just as I laid him down in the bassinet so I could quickly sneak in a shower, a meal, a scroll through Instagram, his eyes would spring open and we'd start the process all over again.

But, eventually, I found that the most effective method was also the worst-looking, and I was glad that so much of early parenthood is a private affair. The sleep-training websites called it "rocking to sleep," but it did not resemble a gentle lullaby. It is firm and aggressive—an exaggerated full-body hiccup timed to a two-step—that's supposed to be combined with swaddling and shushing at the exact volume of a shower, which is a loud volume to try to sustain a shush, the expulsion of breath already depleting a wrung-out brain.

This all happened, of course, while Marc was screaming. He did this with the combined effort of every sinew in his body, and it was louder than anything I expected could come out of something so puny. My mother-in-law sent me a video of a guest on *Oprah* who could decipher newborn cries: If you heard *neh*, it meant they were hungry; a more throaty *aah* meant they had gas. But the sound my baby was making was none of these; he was not soothed by feeding, burping, or singing. In my delirium, his cries sounded existential: *Who brought me here?! I was not asked!*

I knew Qing and Dexin could hear Marc crying from the basement apartment where they were quarantining. She always told my sister and me that we barely cried; meanwhile, my child's wails penetrated through walls. After ten days and two negative tests, Qing rushed in to take over, and I could see, though did not yet appreciate, how she was careful not to criticize or compare out loud, and how she modulated her questions—"Maybe he doesn't like to be holding like that?" I felt the aimless, diffuse frustration inside me turn caustic, blackened by fear and exasperation, and I responded by pointedly ignoring Qing's questions.

A part of me realized what was happening. I was behaving in the exact same way that I once believed was the source of all my unhappiness. It dawned on this rational part of me that Qing had at one point learned that her family would listen to what she was saying if she didn't yell it at them. Had we switched places, me the angry one and she the tiptoer? Had it happened like a tipping point—a final straw that changed everything—or was it like a Cancún sunrise, a little bit at a time, until we were no longer sitting in darkness? I was not in the right state of mind for this realization. It made me angrier, more impatient, more reckless.

Early one evening, as Marc peacefully, unusually, drifted

off to sleep without any aids, Qing wondered aloud if it was because the rocking was more stressful than soothing. "It scaring him," she pondered, though the syntax made it sound like a conclusion.

I chose the least generous interpretation, ready for a fight. I snapped, telling Qing that I knew what I was doing, that it was perfectly safe and fine because I had obviously done my research—something I had hoped my own mom would trust me to have done—and if *anyone* knew what he needed, it would not be someone who had mostly seen him on FaceTime, a daily tradition that I had chosen to initiate only when he was in a good mood.

"At the end of the day, he's *my* son," I seethed.

In the dark, I could not see her face, but I knew that the bomb I'd thrown had detonated. It was too late to take it back, but then again, I also meant it, or at least the most reflexive part of me meant a part of it. I had never before been able to express myself in a fight, to put words to the chaos, or felt brave enough to offer a perspective that could be considered. But was this what I had in mind as a kid? Was this standoff in the dark my idea of independence?

Qing eventually spoke: "I want to go home." She made sure that I understood her. Then she spun on her heels and left the room. I took my time putting Marc down in his bassinet, and he did not wake back up immediately. I stood over him in the dark for a long, long time, trying to remember what exactly I said, and not being able to think of anything beyond the last thing I said, which grew more like a threat with every passing second. He's my son. He's *my* son. He's *mine.*

I passed Dexin on my way to the basement, who looked at me cautiously. "Give her time," he warned.

Qing had locked herself in the bathroom, a small space just big enough to stand in. I could hear her violent gasps.

"Mom, I'm really sorry. Can we talk?"

Heavy breathing.

"I didn't mean to fight with you. I'm just so tired. I explained myself badly."

Heavier breathing.

"Mom."

"I want to go home," she moaned in between gasps.

"Mom, I don't want you to go. I need you here. I—"

"I want to go home," she repeated, not hearing me. "I want to go home. I want to go home."

•

AND HERE is the theme of my life, and of Qing's. Home: the place we return to for solace, and our inability to do so because—always—we are not finding it in places, are never totally comfortable with a language, much less a zip code. But home, it seems, is not even the families we were born into, or the families we made.

I often think about the hours that followed, especially in moments when I feel thunderstruck by my love for Marc, when he laughs and I cannot fathom anything that has existed, or will exist, that will ever be as essential. My son is the first person for whom I've been able to witness this growth of love, and be fully conscious of it, and it is worth describing how it came to be. My love for Marc did not spring from nothingness—nor was it passed through skin-to-skin contact, or some hormonal miracle, or a sense of duty or obligation. He is still so young, and this love I have for him is younger even than that, but I know with great certainty that this love grows from complication and friction, from attending to him and trying to understand him—and knowing that he is doing the same, in his own remarkable, capable ways, for me.

I do not know if that is how everyone loves. But that is how I do it. And during those brief hours when I lay in bed, staring at the monitor of Marc dozing in the next room, I began to see that I would never really understand Qing, and she would never understand me—I hardly understood myself these days, and I knew she was feeling the same.

The point was that we would always continue to try. And that we have always assumed that the other would always try. We will always be trying to find the words. That commitment is as close to a definition of love as I can fathom.

A screech erupted from the monitor. I told Nathan to stay put—it was technically his turn, but I needed to go, and I ventured out of the bedroom.

There she was. Qing was sitting on the armchair outside Marc's room—it looked like she had been there for some time. We both went in without speaking, and fell into small actions, handing blankets and rags back and forth to each other, taking turns rocking, feeding, soothing. Then:

"I'm sorry."

"I am sorry."

Qing took her time to find her words, but once she did it all came out. How it took her twenty years before she finally let go of her anger at allowing herself to get trapped, away from a home she never meant to leave. How it took her years still to understand that her life was not over, that in many ways, it was just beginning. How what I said—"He's *my* son"—rang a primal alarm, and even though she knew I could not have meant what she feared, she couldn't help but see it as a declaration of my ownership and dominance over him—the most bastardized version of love that she never wanted to find herself in, and had always feared she might end up in.

"*I* do not belong to no one," she concluded. Expecting sadness, I reached out to grab her hand, but I saw that she was not sad at all.

Her hands, still stones at her sides, were determined. "I do not belong to a man, to my children. Not a job. Not a country. I do not belong to no person, nowhere, nothing. I am free."

We sat there for some time, watching the sun rise through the window, circling the same thought, a hymn to no god.

How lucky we were, Qing and I, to not belong, together.

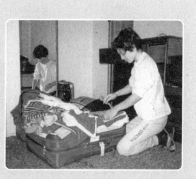

# Acknowledgments

Thank you to Cindy, by way of Mel, whose first conversation with me, during a time in my life when I felt as original as a Shein knockoff, was the catalyst for this book. I think about your magnanimity often.

Thank you to all the brutal, gentle, razor-sharp, deeply weird editors I've had, from blogs to books, who've encouraged me to put myself first, last, in the center, and absolutely nowhere (on the page and otherwise). Each red pen mark has been a gift.

To my editor, Amy Sun, and my agent, Marya Spence, for getting it from the start, which made all the difference. And to Andrea Schulz, Carolyn Coleburn, Johnathan Lay, Christine Choi, Mackenzie Williams, and the entire team at Viking Penguin and Janklow & Nesbit.

I owe my sanity and spirit to my dear friends from the

Hallway, Intern Summer 2008, #4R, and the various group chats whose names I should not put in print. There's so much more to celebrate, plot, and share.

Thank you to my little sister, Julia, who I should apologize to every day for the rest of my life. You have always been the bigger person. I lov you. To Ra Ra for your idealism and sense of responsibility. And, obviously, Ga Ga—you have never been anyone other than yourself. You're a hero and a role model, even though I know you don't want to be either.

Thank you to Donna, for your mothership, too.

And thank you, Nathan, for everything else, everything good, and everything truly important.